It's Never Too Late

by

Barbara Kacer

Bloomington, IN  Milton Keynes, UK

authorHOUSE®

AuthorHouse™
1663 Liberty Drive, Suite 200
Bloomington, IN 47403
www.authorhouse.com
Phone: 1-800-839-8640

AuthorHouse™ UK Ltd.
500 Avebury Boulevard
Central Milton Keynes, MK9 2BE
www.authorhouse.co.uk
Phone: 08001974150

First published by AuthorHouse 7/25/2007

ISBN: 978-1-4343-0096-6 (sc)

Library of Congress Control Number: 2007902425

Printed in the United States of America
Bloomington, Indiana

This book is printed on acid-free paper.

A big thank you to my good friend Doris Jewell, who typed this entire manuscript into the computer from my typewritten original copy, and proofread it at the same time. Also, a sincere thanks to my daughter Yvonne Higashi, who proofread it a second time and sent it off to the publishers. And last but not least, a note of appreciation to Suellen Dehnke who helped with various tasks and was also a seminary wife herself.

I love you gals!

PROLOGUE

MY HUSBAND, AT the age of 38, decided to change the course of his life. This decision involved not only him but our three children and me as well. We were to sell our house and leave the neighborhood in which we had lived for 10 years. For my husband's goal was to become an ordained Lutheran minister and he would be going to school for the next four years.

Share with me the trials, the fears, the hardships, and the joys during our seminary years.

<u>It's Never Too Late</u>

Dedicated to all the women everywhere who are now "sem" wives, or have been, or ever will be.

Barb Kacer 1975

My grace is Sufficient for you – 2 Corinthians 12:9

My husband and I were both 38 years old in September 1973 when he entered the Lutheran Church Missouri Synod Seminary in Springfield, Illinois, to prepare for the ministry. It certainly had not been an overnight decision but it was still a shock when it finally happened. Dan had toyed with the idea for years and I had even encouraged him, but I really never thought he would go through with it.

When we were married in December 1961, he told me he always wanted to become a minister, and had begun his preparation for it as a young boy. Dan attended Whiting High School in his hometown in Indiana for two years, but transferred to Concordia Lutheran in Fort Wayne to finish high school. This was followed by two years of Jr. College in the same city after which he attended the Indiana University Extension at East Chicago for a year. He then completed his Bachelor's Degree at Indiana University in Bloomington.

Because of many factors, one being a previous illness, Dan went to work for the YMCA after graduation instead of continuing his schooling. Yet, eventually he completed courses at George Williams College to become a certified YMCA secretary.

He became involved with youth groups, went on camping excursions, attended teenage dances; in fact, when I met him, it was at the Y and he was surrounded by students. They were preparing a bill to present to the legislature in Springfield, Illinois, and my date, being a law student, was there to help out with any legal problems.

Dan seemed happy then and I guess he was for a while. But after we were married, I knew he was, after all, a frustrated layman that still wanted the ministry.

We spent our first year of married life in Park Forest, Illinois, and Dan continued to work for the Y while I was a nurse at Ingalls Hospital in Harvey. Then, in October 1962, we were blessed with a baby boy, Michael.

Just six weeks later, we moved to Wauwatosa, Wisconsin, where Dan had accepted a new position with the **Y**.

We were settling in, Mike was almost two, and I was pregnant again, when Dan decided it was time to return to Harvey. We bought a house in Riverdale, Illinois (a suburb of Chicago) close to Harvey and were able to move in just in time for Christmas. Yvonne was born in January 1965 and at that time we had joined St. Paul Lutheran Church in Dolton.

We became active in the church, Dan was on the Stewardship Committee and also served as chairman of the Building Committee; their aim was to build a new Lutheran School. I joined the Altar Guild and when Yvonne was three, began teaching Sunday School. Yet Dan never seemed completely satisfied with his role in the church; something was missing.

Then one of our fellow parishioners, who had entered the seminary when he was in his late 30's, was ordained in our church; he had a wife and five children.

It was about that time when Dan began to think about his frustrations and pondered that, "Maybe it's not too late."

We were buying our house, we were settled in a nice neighborhood, and I was working part-time at the hospital. I was content, but Dan was not.

In 1967, we bought a puppy, Tuffy, who grew to be quite large for the children. The same year I became sick with hepatitis, so my hospital career was over for a while.

In June 1969, Dan left the **Y** and began to search. He taught at our Lutheran School for three months, purchased steel, worked for a construction company and, for several weeks, did not have a job at all. So, it was about this time I went back to work part-time at Pronger-Smith Clinic in Blue Island.

In October 1971, when I was 36 years old, our third child, Erika, was born. Although I was a nursing mother, I returned to work after just five weeks because Dan's job at the construction company did not pay enough for us to get by.

Dan tried to enjoy his job and the type of work he was doing, because he had a wife and three children to support, but his heart was not in it. At this point, he said his aim was to earn good money for the family, as he certainly wasn't dedicated to what he was doing.

He asked for a raise right before we went away on a 3-day ski trip to Michigan. After three days of fun, he went back to work, had a few words with his boss and that was the end of his big money making career. That was in March 1973. I continued to work at the clinic while Dan found a few odd jobs. Yet we both knew where we were headed and one day I finally broke the silence.

"Dan, you are not getting any younger. If you want to be a pastor, you better start now." As I spoke I could have bitten my tongue; I loved my life, I was content, but I also knew how he felt.

In April Dan applied for admission to the Missouri Synod Lutheran Seminary in Springfield, Illinois and was accepted in June. Ironically, that summer he went to work for the **Y** until it was time to go away to school.

On September 5, 1973, with a lump in my throat, I watched Dan leave our suburban home for Springfield. We (me and the children) were to stay behind until the house was sold which was to take almost a year. In the meantime I continued to work at the clinic.

Excerpts of Dan's first few letters revealed some of his innermost feelings:

September 11, 1974 (his first letter home)

Dear Barbs:

After two days of classes and some 8 hours additional per day in study, I want to write to tell you I love you, as you know, and miss you and the kids. Thank God that I've been occupied on His Word (and Greek) so that I don't get into dwelling on us not being together.

I pray we will all be together in Springfield soon. That will be quite a celebration. I guess the only way I'm bearing our present situation is knowing that our God is watching over my family, strengthening it, and in His good time will bring us together.

And later in his letter he writes to the children, Mike 10, Yvonne 8 and Erika 2.

To the kids – Mike, I trust you're at least tolerating school and are doing all of your homework, and fish tank, gerbils and garbage, without mom having to holler at you too much. I count on you to see that Yvonne gets home safely after school each day – you're her big brother so watch out for her, I miss you son, wish you were here.

Yvonne (Pookey) I won't say anything about your school work except no more B's, I expect A's from you, just continue to enjoy school, your brother, sister, mom and your friends. I know you are helping your mom out and wish I could sit and hold you in my lap right now.

Erika between your mom, brother and sister I am sure you are slowly getting used to the potty and out of diapers (I hope so). Give Tuffy a dog biscuit and don't forget your daddy who still has a moustache, bostache as you call it, misses you very much.

To all of you your pictures are on my desk so I'm close to you and am reminded of what a super blessing you are to your mother and me. I pray every day that God be with you and help you get as much happiness as possible out of this temporary, and for you too, difficult time of being apart. OK kids back to the TV.

Barbs, any apprehension or doubts about me in seminary training and ministry that may have existed before last week – forget it. THIS IS HAPPINESS. I'm anxious to get out of school as soon as possible because I'm completely humbled to know God wants me as His man.

Most of the other married men had the same difficulty explaining how we got here, apprehension about are we too old to hack it? And other doubts as I did. But once we got off looking at ourselves and simply looked to Christ and His Word we knew.

Love Dan

In his letter of September 15th, Dan talks about looking for a part-time job and then toward the end says, "I sure hope someone is interested in the house because if we can't sell it now we ought to consider renting it out. As I said before, there is almost any kind of housing available in Springfield. I've seen some big houses you would love, but that's rather academic until our house is sold."

"I look forward to the weekend when we'll all be together. I do need a break from the books since after a while, nothing is retained and I get punchy, take a nap and hit them again. I hate to add that after this coming weekend home the length of time between weekends at home with you and the kids will probably get longer. I think I'll be working Friday and Saturday nights until the house is sold and you're all here with me."

Love Dan

Dan was receiving mail in Springfield from us too.

September 19, 1973

Dear Daniel,

I just received your letter, I had a feeling I'd be hearing from you so I waited to write.

Erika is already coloring in the book you sent her. She was excited to get something in the mail. Her swing broke yesterday and I said dad will fix it so she's waiting for you to come home.

What a beautiful first letter you wrote us. I'm glad you're so happy, we're all fine here, but money, as usual, is the problem.

Dr. Pronger gave me ten dollars last week because I drove him to the gas station to pick up his car. He's so generous and good to me. He told me "Use it to buy the kids some hamburgers." But instead I bought myself a long dress.

*Doris and I went out Tuesday morning and each bought a long dress. They're beautiful and inexpensive and we had a ball modeling them for each other.

*Neighbors and good friends Doris & Bob Foyut, who have children that play with our kids.

Tuffy is OK except he's had two accidents in the house since you've left. Maybe he's rebelling, and no, Erika does not go on the potty yet, but she's so good for Mrs. Franchetti, maybe soon.

Your mom called last week and she and grampa are fine. I think my parents will go with us to see them next Sunday.

Maybe you can have my car tuned up when you come home – it needs something.

Well, it's 11 am and Erika and I will mail this now. I need gas in the car and I have to bring Mike his baseball glove as there's softball after school. Then off to work at 1:20.

I'll have the kids write soon.

Love Barb

Sunday September 23, 1973 6:30 pm.

Dear daddy,

I miss you a lot; I wish you would come home. What do you do on weekends? Everybody says hi, even Tuffy. Don't laugh but you just left a few hours ago and I'm righting (Vonnie's spelling) already.

From Vonnie

And in the same envelope

September 24, 1973

Dear Dan

Monday night and I'm watching the 10 pm news. Mike is eating *Malt O' Meal*, Erika is on the couch, she's supposed to be going to sleep and Vonnie is asleep upstairs.

I just got home from work at 9:30 so now to relax for a while. I was at the clinic this morning too; I had to take Vonnie to see the doctor. The rash on her left buttocks was worse and it turned out to be impetigo. I have an ointment to put on it.

Erika won't stay on the couch and Mike is making her wilder, if that's possible. Now he just complained there's a bug in his milk

Guess what? I just checked and there are worms in the powdered milk. Now I won't be able to relax until I've checked all the boxes in the cupboard. Oh well, it needs cleaning anyway.

Last night was awful. I was so depressed when you left us, this time was even worse than the first time. Vonnie kept crying she wouldn't go to the doctor and Mike wouldn't let me do anything to his hair. I was almost hysterical as I tried to cut his hair and so was he.

All three children were in bed by 9 and then I sat down and watched "Funny Girl" during which I had a good cry.Mike finally cut his own hair, somewhat, and I told him if he washed it tomorrow it might be presentable. Erika is still awake, how relaxing my evening has been. She keeps rambling on.

Oh, I almost forgot to tell you about last night. Vonnie was fooling with her buzz board and down it fell. Seconds later a loud crash came from Mike's room as the bottom shelf of his bookcase fell to the floor. What a mess. I really needed you home then.

I love and miss you.
Barb

September 26, 1973
Dear Barbs:
Before I study tonight, I want to share the enclosed letter with you. I've already written a thank you to Mac. What a blessing. (Mac, a fellow member of St. Paul's in Dolton, had written to Dan saying he and his wife would like to send him a modest amount of money each month).

Mac went on to say in his letter "now I know this is not going to alter your financial condition, but it lets you know every month that someone loves you and prays for your success as a pastor."

Dan and I were both deeply touched by this letter and I had to agree with him. He said "this letter is another indication to both of us not to worry or get all strung out over money."

But I was to forget this many times in the month to follow.

September 27, 1973
Dear Dan:
Our letters must have passed in the mail. I deposited 260 dollars on Monday but haven't made a house payment, as I can't find the checkbook.

Last night was very frustrating. I had bunco club here and the kids were well behaved for a change.I played bunco with my life long friend Elaine Ziehm and some of her neighbors Everyone went home about 11:40 and I began to clean up. About midnight, Erika began to cry and to make a long story short; she vomited five times in the next two hours. We were up until after 2 a.m. so you can imagine how I feel today. I had made popcorn for club and Erika had her share. The last time she threw up I discovered a whole shell or husk of popcorn mixed in with everything else. She's OK today.

Vonnie says to tell you she hurt her finger. She's so graceful she fell down the stairs and somehow twisted it. Her rash is much better.

Mike is watching "Kung Fu." We all helped deliver his newspapers tonight. I drove while Mike and Vonnie ran and delivered house to house.

Your sister Amy called tonight and everything is set for your parent's 50th anniversary party next Sunday. I finished Vonnie's shawl so she can wear it to the party, and now I want to make one for my sister's birthday next month.

Well, I just got Vonnie and Erika in their PJ's. There will be no school tomorrow, isn't Mrs. Franchetti lucky?

Study hard and be good. I think of you almost constantly. Erika asked, "Is daddy coming oba (Erika's way of saying over) tonight?" Sure wish you were.

                                                                    Love Barb

P.S. Don't worry about money you say, what happens when we run out?

Parts of Dan's September 29th letter

"Please love, spend some time with the kids, maybe a devotion in the evening or at supper time and remind them I love them and pray for all of you daily. But they need the Word that's the most important thing we've got.

And later in the letter "Included in necessities I would suggest a fine haircut or trim for Mike. His hair is thick and long, he needs firm instruction in keeping it neat. No sense in you and he hassling over hair. Send him (insist he go) to the barbershop on 144th and Clark. He's old enough to go alone and he won't cry there the way he does when we cut it at home."

                                                              October 1, 1973

Dear Dan

I'm writing this from work. Doctor still has five more patients and it's already 9 p.m. so thought I'd start a letter. As I write I can hear it storming outside; hope it stops by the time I go home.

I finished Carol's shawl yesterday in time for her birthday in four days. Now I'm starting one for Amy Jo so she can have one like her mother. Then

I thought I'd make a black shawl for your sister for Christmas; I have all sorts of plans for things to make for the holidays.

I was happy to receive another letter from you today. No I didn't have the car tuned up yet, just can't seem to find the time. We'll talk about the children when you come home. I get so upset even though I try to be calm. Vonnie cries a lot and Mike teases and punches. What fun.

Sure wish you were going to a school close by so we could all be together.

Tomorrow, I'll call Chapman as I haven't heard a word from them. Maybe we should change real estates.

I'm looking forward to the weekend, but will probably feel worse after you leave. Doctor needs me, will write more later at home.

I'm home now and it's 11 p.m. I'm baking blueberry muffins, washing clothes, writing to you and watching TV. See how talented I am?

Well now I just finished writing out the checks for this month's bills so I think I'll go to bed. I'll be counting the days until Friday; how dramatic.

So see you soon and don't study or work too hard.

Love from all
Barb

October 11, 1973

The last part of Dan's letter

"Monday I got my first test in Early Church back a C. Guess I'll have to study more and harder. But I only blew one question and was 4 points away from a B. I'll be extremely happy to maintain a B average, no way an A. The younger guys are too sharp.

By the way I spent some of the money in the Harvey account for a clerical collar, gold collar, and a Greek New Testament."

October 11, 1973

Dear Dan:

As you can see (from the stationery) I'm writing from work again. It seems to be the only place I can find the time. We're busy as we'll be seeing about 17 patients, but I have time in between each one to write a few lines.

Gee, I thought you'd be writing to let me know your phone number. See how fast you've forgotten us or do you have too much homework? Or is it the nursing home that's keeping you so busy?

I received a water bill today for 18 dollars and also a telephone bill a few days ago for the same amount. I'll pay them plus 10 dollars to Master

Charge after I'm paid next week. Tomorrow, I'll go to the bank to make the house payment.

I had a flat tire yesterday, which I noticed on my way home from the store. So Barb Franchetti drove me to work and my dad fixed the flat when he got home from work.

I'll work every day this week including six hours Saturday, so I should be getting a nice paycheck.

I'm home now and Doris is here knitting, she says hi. The kids are all playing in the front room and Erika is singing. She goes on the potty sometimes (thanks to Gram Franchetti) but has gone number two in her pants two nights in a row and it's fallen out on the floor.

Last night, when it happened, Doris and my mom were here and instead of rushing to Erika's aid, they both sat and laughed while yelling to me to quick clean her up.

Mike is giving me a hard time over his fish (Erika spilled ¼ box of food into the tank) his gerbils and his paper route.

I'll close for now. Write soon. I'm going nuts as usual. How about me going away to school or to a rest home for a while and you can keep house and work?

Tuffy says ruff
Mike says hi
Erika sends a kiss
And Vonnie is writing to you

Love Barb

October 11, 1973

Dear Daddy,

Aunt Kay made me another pair of doll clothes. She made me a long dress shawl and a hat.

Mommy is very tired. She's drinking ice tea. I'm making Erika a hat and shawl (I hope).

Every morning Erika asks, "Where is daddy?"

Love Vonnie

October 12, 1973

Dear Daniel

I'm at work - Friday afternoon and I'm not in the mood of working as usual.

We're pretty well caught up with the bills, I deposited your check today putting $42.88 in and keeping $40 for myself for groceries. I put $70 of my check in the bank and paid bills with it on Tuesday. Well, enough business talk.

We had a birthday party for Mike and Erika on Wednesday night with gram and grampa Lindstrom coming over for supper. Then later, Doris, Bobby, and Gail came over for cake and a drink. *Zelda and Mariann didn't come because Wally had his hernia operation this morning. I'm happy to report he's doing well.

Gee, I wish you'd be home Sunday as your family is coming over for still another birthday celebration. I said I'd have cold cuts, cheese and chips.

Now your sister Amy called and said she'd bring lasagna and Jan will make potato salad.

I called Walter's Tin Shop on Tuesday and they came the next day to check on the heat. Something about the heat being blocked by dirt. Do they mean filters? They'll send us a bill. The children enjoyed their birthday cards from you and I liked my card, but would have preferred a letter. But I know you are busy so you can tell me everything when you come home in two weeks. At times like this, two weeks seems like such a long time.

Mike said he'd get a haircut when I get home so I may (as a reward?) let Bobby and little Mike stay over tonight.

Write soon, Love Barb

*Our neighbors across the street and also our fellow parishioners at St. Paul Lutheran; Mariann is Erika's Godmother.

Yvonne faithfully wrote daddy again to enclose with my letter.

October 20, 1973

Dear Daddy:

Today is Saturday afternoon. Grandpa L. got me a second-hand bike. Me, Erika and grandpa are going to grams. I'm going to ride my bike there.

I quit organ lessons. Erika got the stitches out of her head last Saturday.

Erika got lots of presents for her birthday. Mike got presents too. His favorite is from Bobby and Gail. It is a racetrack and motorcycle.

Thanks for the card and it wasn't even my birthday.

Love Pookey

PS - Aunt Amy, Aunt Jan and those guys are coming over tomorrow.

From Dan

I did get some more test results since I wrote you last. An A in a doctrine class (Revelation Scripture) so your husband is holding his own for now anyway with a solid B average.

I'm still hoping that we can sell the house and be together soon rather than wait until June 1974 – that's ages away, Dear Heart. The commuting on weekends is okay but with working at the motel an entire Saturday and Sunday one week and going home the next, I get behind in the very thing I'm here for – to prepare for the ministry.

But with God's help we will do it – somehow, someway.

Many times a whole month would go by before Dan would get home for a weekend.

November 6, 1973

Dear Dan:

At work again, and just time to write a few lines. How was your trip back? I bet you were tired when you got there.

Mike gave me a very hard time Sunday night and Monday morning. It's just like he's testing me and it's hard to bear. For instance, yesterday he didn't want to wear a winter coat and it was 35 degrees. He stayed in his room until 7:50 and I just ignored him. At times I'm hysterical, then I try playing it cool. I don't know if I can stand it much longer. There's nothing new on the house either.

Have you heard anything about Thanksgiving? I sure hope you can come home so you can help cook and do the dishes, etc.

The house insurance bill came today from Corey and Adams. Do I pay it all at once?

Nothing more to say as I just saw you two days ago. I miss you, especially on cold nights.

Love Barbs

Dan again lamented about our being apart.

November 10, 1973

"What we're experiencing is maintaining two places of residence. In other words, if we were all living together under one roof, it would take less money. That hurts not only financially but also emotionally. I miss you and the kids.

But I want you to understand how I've put the situation into proper perspective. Read Proverbs 31: 10-13. It says better than I can how I feel about you."

After turning to my Bible and reading the suggested passages I was shocked. Why it spoke of an almost perfect woman. I was nothing like that, how could Dan be so blind?

I was restless, resentful and I shouted at the children too often when I came home from work. Maybe I should keep reading this passage, it was something to work towards.

November 12, 1973

Dear Dan,

Here I am at work - my long Monday. We're just busy enough as the time is going fast.

I received your letter today and see you wrote it right before you went to work on Saturday. I tried to call you on Saturday as I have several things to tell you.

First of all, we will be coming to Springfield next Saturday. We are going to my sister's house (Havana) but we'll stop there first. We'll arrive about 12:30. Will you meet us by the office at the motel? Let me know.

Next, Pastor Marquardt called on Friday night and said he thought the church could help you financially this next quarter. I told him you still need 480.00. Is that right?

Gram Kacer called yesterday to see how everyone was. She told me "We're old. We have our home, so we will help you all we can." I told her they've helped us enough but she insists next time I come over she'd help some more.

Well, I'll close now and eat my supper (a sandwich).

Love Barbs

P.S. Home now and Mike is really acting up. Pastor M just called – they voted to send you a grant of 500 dollars. He'll be putting it in the mail tomorrow.

Love Again

November 26, 1973

Dear Barbs,

I put the typed Christmas letter in the mail on Wednesday so you should get it with this letter. I think we'll need about 100 copies made.

I'm scheduled to work every weekend through and including December 15th, so it doesn't look like I'll be home until Thursday December 20th (Christmas vacation until Jan 7). Sorry I won't be able to get home sooner unless something unexpected happens. That's only four weeks away and in the meantime I'll get Michael's gift – a fancy, heavy wood carved chess set and book. I'll have more on that in the next letter.

Roy and Joy (couple with whom Dan lived for a short while) appreciated the goodies from home. I also shared some with Jim Cooley's family.

So, St. Paul congregation (all the wonderful people) are being thanked by three families.

Oh yes, I'm writing to pastor today – also the thank you to the congregation for the food shower and will pick up several more thank you cards for the Altar Build, Ladies Aid, The Bochmanns (Wally and Zelda) at the bookstore.

You know how much I love you and miss you and the kids.

Yours in Christ Dan

We had been so generously dealt with by friends and organizations from our home church at Thanksgiving time. It was overwhelming.

November 29, 1973

Dear Daniel,

I sure don't feel like writing to someone who isn't coming home for three more weeks. How icky for me to be alone to get everything ready for Christmas. Also I'm sick of cleaning house every week, only to have it get dirty again. Now that I have some complaining off my chest I feel a little better.

I worked today, but I'm off tomorrow so will try to do a little Christmas shopping. Also I gave my dad our Christmas letter to have copies made so should have them out by next week.

The TV man came on Wednesday and we needed three new tubes. It cost 28 dollars so it's good we held off on the house payment.

I had Mike and Vonnie write Christmas lists last night. I'll try not to charge anything. Will you be sending me a check? It's hard to make my check cover bills, food and Christmas.

Well A student, keep studying and be good.

See you in three weeks – Love Barbs

P.S. We'll wait until the 20th to get a tree, as you're so good at picking them out.

Our Christmas letter written by Dan
Christmas 1973
In celebration of our Lord's Birth, Merry Christmas and a Blessed New Year to you.

By God's Grace, His Holy Spirit has worked many wonders in the Kacer Family this past year. We humbly share them with you, so that you too may experience His love and power.

Dan is at the Seminary in Springfield, Illinois, preparing for the office of the Holy Ministry. By God's Grace, he is humbly subjecting himself to His Word and Will so that he can joyfully share the Gospel with all. It is proving to be a real experience in how God's love works in a very personal way. A sense of urgency to graduate grows daily. Academically all goes better than expected, especially since part-time work occupies precious moments, but it is necessary.

Barbara continues to work at the Pronger Smith Clinic on a part-time basis. Although at times the work and kids get to her she is content as usual, with her lot and looks for the day our home at 14313 Wallace is sold. Then our entire family will be together in Springfield.

Michael, 11, is emerging as an excellent basketball player and does well at school. His interest and knowledge of chess causes some good games with Dan. Mike is the little man of the house while dad is away.

Yvonne, 8, continues to amaze everyone by her excellence at school, her many talents and beautiful personality. Who's prejudiced? She is her daddy's Pookey and takes care of her sister Erika.

Erika, just 2 years old, is the little "love bug" of our family. She cares for her puppy (he's 7 years old) Tuffy by feeding him dog biscuits constantly and sharing her food with him.

Dan's mom and dad celebrated their 50th wedding anniversary in October. We are especially grateful to our Heavenly Father for their precious ways and holding good health.

Barb's mom and dad continue to be there when needed (and more). Helen still works but finds plenty of time for her grandchildren. LeRoy also works and spends not only hours with the children, but also doing things like maintaining cars and our home. Thank God for his skills because Dan can only assist him.

All in all as we approach another Birthday of our Lord Jesus Christ, we simply say His Grace has brought us closer to His Cross. For that we are grateful and pray that you too will experience His Love in abundant measure and wish you a Merry Christmas and a Blessed New Year.

In Christ the family of Daniel J. Kacer
Dan, Barb, Mike, Vonnie and Erika

December 2, 1973 7:45 pm

Dear Barbs:

I have a short break from studying so will write a few lines.

Enclosed is my check, not much but I was home for Thanksgiving. I've already worked three shifts this week and will work Friday, Saturday and Sunday this coming weekend. So, the next one should be more like 90 dollars. (Around Dec. 15).

I wrote a thank you note to the Altar Guild, Ladies Aid and also wrote a letter of thank you to the congregation for publication in January's newsletter.

I got Mike a chessboard and wooden pieces as well as a book as I said I would. Such a deal I couldn't pass it up. I hope we'll be able to play by mail. I'll explain when I get home.

This quarter is only one week old and I can tell it's going to be harder than the fall quarter. So I better try to get some reading done.

Love to you and the kids – you're in my thoughts and prayers daily

Miss you In Christ, Dan

PS I'll be home late on the 20th, last class gets out at 3:15. I'll be driving 50 mph. We can get the tree on the 21st if that's not too late for the kids.

December 8, 1973

Dear Dan:

I'm at work today 10 to 4 and am starting this on my lunch break. We're doing ok except I think Mike and Erika are getting colds.

Your sister is picking up the kids at 12:30 today to take them to her Christmas Party at work. Erika is looking forward to it and says she's going with aunt KO (KO is my brother-in-law).

I went to Mike's basketball game last night and he's really good. They won 23-13 (that's 3 in a row now) and Mike scored 18 points. I still have Christmas gifts to buy but as you can imagine I'm out of money. My mom gave me 30 dollars added to what I already owe her. She bought Mike and Vonnie snow boots (we had snow here last week yeah) and yesterday she bought Mike two pairs of pants. His 12's are getting too small.

We're starting hours again so will close

Love Barb

Suddenly all our plans changed because my niece Karen was getting married on December 21st in Havana, Illinois, and Springfield received several inches of snow on the 19th so the Sem closed a few days earlier than expected. Dan decided to go directly from school to Havana, as it was only 50 miles away. We'd go to Havana with my parents and meet him there and then we'd all go home together on the 22nd.

Dan ended his letter of 12-14

"All goes well even with an overload of class hours. All that is missing is you and the kids.

I have leads on several homes that have fireplaces, no steep stairs and are in town. With the gas shortage (or price of gas) I guess you'll have to wait (or forget) a home in a small country town.

Love to all – see you in Havana
Dan

January 13, 1974

Dear Dad,

We had a lot of snow. There are big snow hills down at the corner. Dawn and me played on them Thursday night. After that, we went to Sears. Grandpa got shirts and Mike got a knew (Vonnie's spelling) pair of shoes.

Grandpa left for California Saturday morning. Mom had car trouble that night so Mr. Foyut came over to fix the car.

Everyone misses you a lot
Love Pookey

January 14, 1974
Dear Daniel,

Gee, you really must miss us; you keep in touch so closely. Now I know I haven't written either but I think you have a little more time than I.

Enough preaching – how are you? I took my driving test today (written) and of course, I'm an A student, just like you. I admit that I do miss you, but after two days, we'd be fighting again. Erika again said last night, "I want daddy to come over." She has to tell everyone on the phone, "My daddy's at Jesus School." Mike's team won both games this week. Friday he scored 2 points and on Sunday 10 points.   Come home soon.

Love Barb

Our letters crossed in the mail again as Dan wrote:

January 13, 1974

Dear Barbs,

As you can tell I'm at work (by the stationery) and am studying for one of two tests. I should have taken them before Christmas but didn't because of the snow and school closing early.

For some reason, maybe because I'm looking forward to having you and the kids here by June, this winter quarter is strange. Other than work and study there is nothing to do. No nursing home, no hospital yet, hopefully later this month. Maybe because I get up at 6:30, go to class when it's still dark – whatever I'd just like to have all of us together, roll in the snow, ski with the kids.

In many respects I feel like a monk, but that I'm not. So please write with some good news about the house.

By the way, as I mentioned before, many houses are available in and around Springfield, reasonable too. Maybe you'd like to come down for a weekend?

Well, I better close and get to work. How are Mike and his basketball? Yvonne and her overnights? Erika and her Tuffy? Instead of beating them tonight, give them all my love.

I Miss you and I need you with me
In Christ Dan

February 10, 1974

Dear Barbs,

At work again, Sunday night – only 15 rooms rented out of 100 so it's not all that busy.

Be sure to tell the kids to include me in their prayers, especially for this Thursday's Greek test. I failed it the first time and would be terribly behind if I fail again.

Gee wish you and the kids were here and we had our home together. It would make everything much easier and more fun.

Erika is something else huh? Writes letters and looks for me in the am. For her sake I hope we're not separated too much longer; otherwise, she'll be confused.

Is basketball over? No news about the longhaired whiz kid? Guess I'll have to wait a few weeks to show him a few things about alley basketball. Miss him even though I know he acts like a brat (at times).

How about Yvonne? Is she still a super scholar and a tomboy – or more of a lady like her mother? I guess she and Mike are so wrapped up in school and friends; they don't have time to write. They are normal and I hope they enjoy everything they are doing. Once they get here it will be looking forward to new friends, new schools, new places. Golly it must scare them to look forward to that. I hope not because we can share it together.

Don't worry about me catching the flu. I thought I was coming down with it so I fought it with my three standards, tea, soup and toast and went to bed at 3 p.m.

Love and miss you much
Daniel

February 14, 1974

Dear Daniel

Even though you'll be getting this a few days late, Happy Valentine's Day.

The children are sick with the flu. Vonnie started with it last Saturday, had a cough, fever and sore throat. Mike complained of a headache Sunday night and he's still home with a fever. Erika got sick yesterday morning, vomiting, fever, etc. She then coughed most of the night so I took her to the doctor this morning. She is getting an antibiotic and her lungs are okay.

Grandpa Lindstrom brought us all Valentine goodies. I got a beautiful box of Fannie Mae's with a red ribbon in a pink satin box. The kids got the same, just a smaller box. They are yummy and just what I need.

The Real Estate has been showing the house quite a bit, but to no avail. I guess nobody wants our little kitchen. Last Saturday six couples came to look, maybe one of these times.

I'd better close as Erika feels warm, Von is still coughing and Mike and I have to change all the water in his fish tank tonight. He's already started.

I love you and can't wait until you come home next week. I'm looking forward to our being together in Springfield but not to getting a new job.

Love Barb

We had changed Real Estates and our house was finally sold at the end of February. One of those six couples did want it. Unfortunately, they had FHA financing so we were still in for a long siege of waiting.

March 25, 1974

Dear Dan,

Well, FHA finally came last Thursday morning. The man looked over everything so quickly I don't know how he could have checked everything. I haven't heard anything since then.

Also, on Thursday Tuffy got out of the yard. He was gone about an hour and then came to the back gate. I called him and he ran the other way. I was all dressed for work and gram had Erika so I got into the car and chased him down several alleys. Then I parked by the post office and as he ran across 144th, I chased him on foot for 3 blocks. I never did catch him, but I was gasping for breath (what great shape I'm in) and my legs felt like they had lead weights on them.

I called Doris before I had to leave for work and she said she'd watch for him. Guess what? Within a half hour your dog was home. He came right up to Doris in front of her house. Isn't he a doll?

Sure wish you were coming home this weekend.

Love Barb

April 2, 1974

Dear Daniel,

Boy I sure loved your long letter so here's one for you too. The Real Estate called on Sunday. FHA said we're to scrape the paint off the back porch and put on one new coat. Also we have to have someone inspect the furnace and the roof.

They'll call you about this when you get home on Friday – won't do anything before then.

Love Barb

Dan had a lead on a Baptist parsonage but on May 2, he wrote:

Dear Barbs:

The Baptist Church is offering the parsonage (1st) to another family in greater need. If they accept we will have to work something else.

Also there is a seminary owned house, but just available June 1 – August 15, that we could have for sure. Although it would require another move in August, at least we'd be together. Oh yes, rent $70 a month, three bedrooms and right across the street from the administration building, which means I could walk to school.

I'm continually praying that you and the kids are reading the Bible and trying to live by our faith. I look forward to the day we do it together. Thank God for your strength and tolerance.

I wish you were here

In Christ Dan

And I wrote at the same time

May 2, 1974

Dear Daniel,

I'm assuming you haven't heard about the house yet – or the news isn't good or you would have called me. The painter and his two sons finally came yesterday and did all the required painting. The back porch really looks good.

The roofer called and said he'd be here on Saturday. So after that we just wait on FHA again.

When are you coming home? If it's still May 23rd, that's three weeks from today. I hope you'll be sending us some money soon as I have a few bills I couldn't pay. Also I have nothing saved for the coming house payment.

Love Barb

Somehow, the house payment was always made as were all the other bills paid.

May 18, 1974

Dan,

Just talked but thought I'd add a few things in a letter. My weekends are so long and hard with the kids. Gram took them to the show this afternoon – that helped.

There are so many things to be done around the house. I'm tired of always depending on my dad.

Let me know what's happening as far as your schedule, etc. I'll wait to give notice at work after I hear from you.

May 21, 1974

Barbs,

My last letter as a young man, the next one will be from the viewpoint of an older more mature? 39 years old. Finally caught up to you.

But we're too old to change now right? So will have to grin and bear the future. We've had many memories to look back on but I'm looking forward to the future with you and the kids in our new calling.

I'll definitely be home on the 29th for our church picnic plus a few days rest and recuperation before summer classes start on June 3rd. Finals are over, I have one more worship service to write and I'm done for the quarter. Looking back it seems like just yesterday we were anxiously awaiting the sem's reply to my application – remember?

There is lots of rain here. I imagine up in Chicago too. Guess a lot of Mike's ball games have been rained out. Say hello to him and remind him of what I expect him to do for you when I'm not around. Like – listen to you – not be a brat – take care of his sisters, etc.

Give my love to Pookey and Erika. See you, the sooner the better.

Love Dan

Our house was sold, everything had gone through and we still had no place to live in Springfield. So at the end of May my parents (for the second time), took me and the children to the State Capital to house hunt. We stayed at the Downtowner where Dan worked.

Dan first of all took us to see a sem house – just 50 dollars a month, but it was unbearable. It was small with only two bedrooms, which we could have tolerated, but because of all the spring rain the basement had flooded and the entire house smelled of mildew.

Then, a real estate took us to see several houses. What we could afford to rent or buy were so bad I became sick.

Next door to the Downtowner was a lot selling house trailers. They were new and clean, so much nicer than the smelly old houses. We looked at several and left Springfield with the understanding Dan would continue to look at trailers, especially second hand ones.

June 5, 1974

Dear Barbs,

I'm at work, only got in 32 hours this week and that's not enough. You'd love my daily schedule – up at 6, class 7:30-9:30, chapel, study until noon, nap (short) study until 3, then work until 11:30. I'm on a 5-1/2 hour sleeping schedule but the nap helps. I'm working on a sermon on

Ep 2:19-22 (which I will preach someday at St. Paul's).

Is there anything new from FHA? That new trailer still hasn't been sold, the used one with central air conditioning turned out to be a 2 bedroom one. However, there will be more used ones coming in and I'll look them all over.

Hi to the children. Love you all and am praying and patiently waiting for news which will bring us together again and enable us to do His will.

In Christ Dan

The children and I really had our hearts set on living in a trailer. We'd have to get rid of a lot of furniture, but it would be fun. Then a few days after his June 5th letter, Dan called.

It was a Thursday night and he had found us a house. He wondered, "Could we come down that next night?"

My parents, the children and I were there by Friday night and I had to admit, even though I was set on a trailer, it was almost ideal. The house, located just four blocks from the sem, had three large bedrooms, a bath, and a study (or a sewing room?) upstairs, while a large living room with a fireplace, a dining room with built-in cabinets and a good sized kitchen covered the first floor. And there was a big screened in front porch.

Of course, there were a few problems. It was an old house, quite dirty and smelly and it was in an old, changing fairly run-down neighborhood. And in regards to the screened in porch, I should have said partially screened, because many of the screens were ripped and the front porch door needed repair.

But – who could be fussy? No indeed this house was within our budget too at 88 dollars a month. We had a place to live.

June 14, 1974

Dear Barbs

Your letter got here yesterday. That's a super Father's Day present – you'll be here around July 1st. I've already moved in from the dorm (yesterday) and had the water, electric, gas and phone turned on.

I know you'll be here next weekend and I'm anxious. Bring the desk from the front room with you if you can. That will help my study.

I've got to get busy and complete two sermon outlines plus type one of them for Tuesday. But I love the course (Sermon Theory) and will probably love Sermon Delivery even more.

Glad to hear Mike won his game. Hope you're being your very patient self with our three blessings who at times behave almost as bad as their father.

Love you much   Dan

June 15, 1974

Dear Dan,

I got your letter and much needed check today. I'll pay some bills tonight.

We are planning to come down Friday night and do not know whether you're working or not, so will stop at the motel first.

Still haven't heard from the FHA on the final adjustments. It seems all we do is wait.

I can't imagine us getting by with my not working and you only 15 hours – will we do it?

We're planning to go to my sister's house on Sunday and will leave Vonnie there for a few weeks. Erika has tonsillitis otherwise everyone is okay.

We'll bring your desk (in my dad's van) and also the bookcases from the family room. I even have some curtains for your study. At least we can get that room in order.

See you Friday night   Barb

THE BIG
MOVE

AFTER SEVERAL WEEKENDS of cleaning and moving some furniture, we made the final move on July 13, 1974. Our neighbors, friends and relatives were so generous in helping us move at the Riverdale end and, of course, gram and gramps Lindstrom came with us to Springfield where there were several sem students available to help us unload and get the furniture in place.

Doris, Zelda and I had sat on Zelda's porch and cried as the final load was put on the truck in Riverdale. My life would never be the same. Moving to Springfield would put us closer to my sister in Havana and I'd always see my parents, but I'd miss Dan's family, our neighbors, and my relatives left in Chicago. I'd miss Elaine and bunco, my cousin Gail Klimke and my old life. At this point, I also knew how much I'd miss my friends Betty and Irene Cummings, whom I've known since I was 4 years old.

Betty, Irene, their mom Bess and bachelor uncle Hank had moved to Riverdale, just a few miles from us, just a couple years before. So, I was able to see them more often and when Erika was born, we took the baby to see them often.

I first met Betty and Irene in 1939 when we moved to 112th Place in Roseland from a rental house on 117th Street. My mom and dad were buying a house this time with the help of grandma Mary Decker. My grandpa Peter Decker had died that same year.

My first recollection of our new neighborhood was of seeing two young girls pushing doll buggies. But they were leaning heavily on the buggy handles and seemed to be dragging their feet. They lived just two doors away from us so we became acquainted right away.

We found out they lived in the upstairs flat of their house with their mom, Uncle Hank, and Grandma and Grandpa Brondyke. Bess told us they had both contracted polio when they were infants and Irene also had cerebral palsy.

Because they were sisters, we always ran their first names together as if they were one person, but they were most certainly two personalities. Betty, the oldest, was about 12 when we met, had dark hair and was serious and even sad at times. In fact, years later, when I had pushed Betty up to Michigan Avenue and we were window shopping, she confessed to me sadly, "I know I'll probably never be able to get married."

Irene, on the other hand, had red hair and at 10 was silly and fun. She stuttered frequently when she spoke but that didn't stop her. Often she had slight tremors. But we always teased her about certain boys and she loved to laugh. But, in later years, she became quite melancholy.

The girls continued for several years to drag themselves up the porch stairs and Carol and I could even pull them in a wagon. But eventually they were confined to their wheelchairs.

Bess worked full-time at Sherwin Williams and was a young, attractive woman of about 34 then. Her parents and brother helped her with the girls as her husband had left the scene years before.

Betty and Irene had to be up early each morning so their mom could get them ready for the day before she went to work. They both attended a special school through the eighth grades; I remember a bus picking them up each weekday morning. But after that they just stayed home, as there were no other provisions for further education for them in the 40's. The girls sat outdoors most of the day during the summer and when we kids all congregated, it was usually at their house or ours. When we jumped rope they'd turn the rope and would love to watch us play Hopscotch and Rolly Polly. They'd help us have a lemonade stand and when it was getting dark they were happy to watch us play Hide-N-Seek. When it was time for them to go indoors, their uncle or grandpa would come and carry them up to the porch and then up the long flight of stairs to their apartment. In the meantime several of us boys and girls would fight over who would get to ride in the wheelchairs as we'd wheel them into the backyard and put them under the porch. Eventually, we learned to take turns instead of fighting over the wheelchairs and only later did we realize how much the girls would have loved to never ride in these chairs again.

Some days Betty and Irene were outdoors quite early and they'd call for us to come and play but it was summer and lazy Carol and I would sometimes sleep until noon. At those times, our grandma Mary would sit out on our front porch on the swing and visit with them. When we'd finally get up and outside, my mom always said, "Go out and blow the stink off you" and we'd go out and the girls would still be waiting. They always liked it if Carol and I would take them for a walk and I feel badly now that we didn't take them on long walks very often. In fact, I teased them and would say, "I'll take you around the block" and then push the wheelchair around one little square block in the sidewalk.

On one rare occasion when I had taken Irene several blocks away, a strange man came up to her and said, "I'm your father." She seemed flustered but didn't say a word to him and he walked away. I felt so sad for both of them.

During the winter Carol and I would visit Betty and Irene in their upstairs flat and everyone would treat us royally. We'd play games; they had so many. I especially remember "Elsie the Cow." We colored and sometimes we would have lunch with them, with grandpa Brondyke praying in his native tongue. Or, we'd have hot chocolate and then, if the girls were tired, they would lay their heads on the dining room table and take a nap while Carol and I continued to play.

One summer day when I was a young teenager my friend Beatsie and I took the girls down the hill to Palmer Park for a picnic. Going downhill was a breeze as we went down at 111ᵗʰ Street where there was a sidewalk without steps sloping down the hill. So Beatsie and I each pushed a wheelchair down into the park. Coming back was another story and we knew it would take both of us to push one chair and girl up the hill. We pushed Irene up first leaving Betty down at the bottom of the hill. We left Irene in front of the clothing store, **Three Sisters,** which was right on the corner.

It didn't take us more than 10 minutes to get back up the hill to Irene. When we approached her we couldn't believe our eyes. She wore a full shirt and her lap was full of change. We laughed as Irene tried to explain to us how surprised she was when people began to throw money in her lap. By then we were laughing so hard we were crying and were wondering how much she would have made if we left her there for an hour!

In later years when I was out of school and working at Roseland Community Hospital I'd walk home from work only to find Irene waiting for me at our corner. Now this meant she had wheeled herself, with no gloves, almost a full block. Her hands were always full of blisters but she loved doing this. I guess it made her feel independent. She and Betty also thought everything Carol or I said was so funny that we sometimes felt like comedians.

Around that same time I began the tradition of baking cookies with the girls, at their house, a few weeks before Christmas. Grandma Brondyke was gone by now but grandpa was still fixing us lunch. It was always early (about 11 am) when he stopped our cookie making to tell us that lunch was ready. The girls would scold him and tell him it was too early but he was just always anxious to show us his hospitality; he was such a fine, loveable man. He always reminded me of Edward Everet Horton, a popular supporting actor of the 30's and 40's.

As the years went by we continued the tradition even when Michael was a little boy of two. How we would laugh when Mike, in awe of grandpa, would follow him around the house even holding his hands clasped behind his back as he imitated everything he did.

Betty and Irene also came to my wedding and the reception even though we had a snow and ice storm that day which was December 9, 1961. A year later their aunt Teen and uncle Ed drove them all the way up to Wauwatosa, Wisconsin with Bess to visit us and baby Michael. They were such a part of our lives and we have such a history. I know they are sad we are leaving Riverdale and I am too. They now sit outside in their neighborhood and watch the young kids play; they are not a part of the gang anymore.

I vow to keep in touch with them and will visit frequently when I'm in the area. Mom and dad live just a few miles from them so it'll be no problem.

So now, after almost 10 years of living in the same area we were beginning a new phase in our lives. I tried to tell myself to "Face everything as an adventure." So I left the south side of Chicago numb, but ready to face new things; or so I thought.

My mom stayed with us that first week. She and Erika took a lot of walks while I scrubbed floors. The rest of the house had been fairly well cleaned on weekends before we moved in. Then my dad joined us on the weekend. My dad and mom sewed, by hand, all the porch screens. What an improvement! The final touch came when dad put up a new porch swing, bought with money I received from Dr. Pronger when I left the Pronger Smith Clinic.

Our house was the second one from the corner. Also there was a small cottage behind the corner house. All three houses shared a big back yard (all houses were owned by the same person) but we fenced ours off because of Tuffy.

Right after we moved in one of our first guests was our niece, Jan and her fiancé, Jerry Hurley. They had been shopping in Springfield coming from Havana (50 miles away) and decided to drop in. Now the house was in chaos with boxes all over, piled up furniture etc. so when Jan asked how things were going, I just motioned to the mess and screamed.

The first night after my mom went home, I cried for my old life but gradually I began to adjust. I met a few other sem wives (many were gone for the summer quarter) and our neighbors, the McCormick's, who lived on the corner side of the duplex next door.

The apartment toward us was vacant, as the couple that lived there had left on vicarage the month before. It would sit empty for two more months until another couple, the Riske's and their baby, would move in after finishing up their vicarage. They had lived there a year before and were willing to pay three months rent without occupancy in order to secure it. Mac and Stella McCormick explained this to us. The McCormick's were probably a little older than my own parents and they became very dear to us in their role as foster parents. They were kept quite busy watching over all the sem families that came and left each year (all those living in the three houses that is).

My mom went back to Dolton one week and was back the next bringing Mike home with her. He had stayed behind with Doris and her family to finish out his baseball season. To my surprise she also brought Doris, Bobby and Gail to stay overnight. Vonnie was home from Havana by then and was thrilled to show Gail her new house.

At that same time another family (the Zielers) from Riverdale were in Springfield. They stayed at a motel as we were quite crowded, but shared a few meals with us. So how could I be lonesome?

In August another neighbor, Vonnie's girlfriend Pam, came by train for a two-week vacation. During her stay important history was in the making as one hot afternoon the announcement came on TV – Richard Nixon was resigning as President of the United States.

So the summer went quickly. When the house was in order, I had loafed around in the sun (what a switch from running to work every day). I worried about getting another job when school started.

Not knowing any other children in town, the kids were quite restless and even anxious for school to start. Dan was still working at the Downtowner Motel and fortunately they had a swimming pool. The kids would go there to swim whenever they wanted (which of course was every day).

We made new friends in other sem families, the Wentzels, Lorna and Wayne, and their three children. Also, the Cooleys, Jim and Betty, and later when school started at the seminary, many, many more. At the beginning of September, Lois and John Riske moved back in next door with their baby Mike, who was almost a year old. We became acquainted right away and had a lot of questions to ask them about their vicarage as ours was drawing near.

Lois and I became very close friends and were together often in the next 10 months in Springfield. She watched Erika for me and I in turn would keep Mike whenever needed. We shopped together and were always looking for food bargains. We ran together around our large yard with Mike and Erika trailing behind. We also shared the ups and downs of being a sem wife. Lois told me, "We're sem students and not quite like regular people." I was to find out what she meant by that.

Before we moved my mother had offered to give me money each month to stay home with Erika. It wasn't hard to accept, but I still took odd jobs where I could take Erika with me. I babysat for individuals, for schools and clubs. It wasn't difficult to find a job through the seminary's daily paper called *The Soup Scoop*. Of course, some of the jobs were weeks apart and only for one time, but every little bit helped. I also cleaned house and babysat every week for a widower with two young boys. I was beginning to realize what Lois had said was right; I didn't feel like regular people. Lois babysat too and because she had only one child she'd go away to take care of children 3-5 days at a time while the parents went on trips. John would join her at night, after classes, so this really worked out well for them. One sem wife gave organ lessons (Vonnie took lessons from her) and sold Avon. Another wife sold Tupperware (I had a party) and she, like me, was a nurse.

FIELD WORK

DAN WAS DOING his fieldwork, obtaining practical experience in the church by working with the pastor, reading the lessons on many Sundays, and in Dan's case preaching just once, at Trinity Lutheran Church, so we enrolled the children at its school. Trinity Church in downtown Springfield was located across the street from the Capital Building. The school was several miles away outside town. I always felt a little awed every time I would look across at this big building and secretly I'd look for a glimpse of the governor or some other famous politician.

I grew to love Springfield even though with a population of around 95,000 it sometimes seemed like a small town. As the state capital, I found it to be a town full of history, especially revolving around none other than Abe Lincoln. One never visited Springfield without going to Lincoln's home, his tomb, and New Salem State Park, where Lincoln, as a young man, lived and worked in a general store. This park consists of replicas of the log cabins making up the village of New Salem. It has a post office, a general store, a school and many homes, one of which houses a doctor's office. Yet as many times as I've been there (my sister lives in Havana just 30 miles away) I still get an eerie feeling thinking that Abraham Lincoln had walked these same paths.

As the time passed we all became very fond of our new church and our fellow members. We looked forward to coming back to it in our 4th year, but it wasn't to be.

THE
SEMENETTES

THE SEMINARY OFFERED classes to the wives taught by the same professors that taught our husbands. What a privilege for us. I really enjoyed both the classes I took; "The role of the Minister's Wife" taught by Professor Henry Eggold and "Parables of Jesus" by Professor M. Steege. By going to classes every Tuesday for 10 weeks, for each course, I had a chance to meet other wives. Also once a month, after classes, the student's wives held their meetings. I'll admit I wasn't too enthusiastic about attending because I felt I was too removed. I had missed my husband's first year and also felt too old. I tried to participate in the helpful projects that were initiated. There always was an opportunity to bring a meal to a needy family in the seminary, to baby sit, visit the sick or shut in, or help a new mother.

DAN'S MUSTACHE

A FEW MONTHS after Dan entered the seminary, he began to grow a mustache. I'll admit I thought it looked good on him at first but after a while it began to aggravate me. He'd stroke it almost all the time and wasn't even aware of it. So he promised to get rid of it when we joined him in Springfield, but after three weeks he was still wearing it. Then one morning (to my surprise) he shaved it off without a word. Only later did I find out why. Apparently in his Sermon Delivery class he had seen a video TV tape of himself and he had noticed that while he preached he continuously played with his mustache.

F I R S T
P R E A C H I N G
A S S I G N M E N T

IN AUGUST, DAN announced "I'm finished with my Sermon Delivery class and now I'm ready to take a preaching assignment." I didn't feel ready but the next day he had an assignment. So we were up early Sunday morning – destination Farmersville, Illinois. This is a small town just 15 miles outside Springfield and the church had been without a pastor for quite a while. So they were used to students.

To my thrilling amazement Dan not only knew how to conduct a service, all by himself, but he also knew how to preach. But I must say the children and I had a few nervous minutes as the service began. Thank goodness no one else knew it was his first time to preach in public. Dan had only one problem with his first sermon (in my opinion). He didn't know how to end his sermon. Twice I thought he was coming to the conclusion – the third time he finally did.

After the service the congregation was receptive and friendly. Several of the people came to me and asked, "Are you the pastor's wife?" I felt so strange. Then a couple representing the congregation took us out for lunch. I told Dan that evening, "If you don't go any further in school this experience has been worth it all."

At the end of August Dan took an assignment at a church 70 miles away in Strassburg, Illinois. In September, we again went to a Strassburg but this time it was in Missouri. This church was 170 miles away so we were to stay overnight. We stayed with a member of the congregation and his family on a farm. The kids were thrilled as they had never really been on a farm (little did we know we'd live on one during vicarage). This was a dairy and hog farm and before church Dan and the kids were up early with the farmer to help feed the cows; I preferred an extra hour's sleep. After the service (there were only about 50 members in the congregation) we enjoyed a delicious dinner and fellowship with this gracious couple that had taken us into their home.

I told Dan later I felt like an imposter, what had we done to be treated so well? And he was paid for each time he preached too!

WE'RE
ADOPTED

AS A FAMILY, a church in Delavan, Illinois adopted us just before Christmas. Each family, when entering the seminary could put their name on a list from which the different congregations could choose. Dan had put ours on at the end of his first year. Being adopted meant the church would help our family by sending us a modest amount of money each month and in our case we also were given a gift of money on our birthday and on Christmas. The Dulevan congregation invited us to a Sunday night potluck and talent show a few weeks after our adoption. This gave us a chance to meet some of the people and to our surprise they also gave us a food shower that night. Of course there were several farmers in the congregation so we not only received canned goods but fresh meat. Delavan, a town of about 2000, is located 50 miles from Springfield so we did try to go back to visit a few times after that first time. Dan also had the privilege of preaching there one Sunday when their pastor was on vacation.

We were getting the feel of the small towns and I loved it, especially after living in Chicago all my life. So we were happy to learn, while out on vicarage, that the Delavan Ladies Aid had decided to adopt us for the remainder of our schooling.

A
TRAUMATIC
BIRTHDAY

OUR SCHOOL YEAR seemed to be divided up by all the holidays. Thanksgiving and Christmas were so close together, yet for each of these occasions as soon as Dan and the kids were out of school, we packed up and went home. Most of the other sem students did the same thing if they lived within a few hundred miles.

By home I'd mean my parent's home in Dolton, with Riverdale next to it. From there we could visit Dan's parent's in Whiting, Indiana, his brother and sisters and their families in Hammond and Highland. Our pastor at Trinity Church, Dr. Niemoeller, always corrected me when I would say, "We're going home" referring to Dolton. "Your home is where your family is," he'd tell me. I knew he was right but wherever we'd venture I still thought of the south side of Chicago as my home.

After Christmas the time until Easter seemed so long and was sometimes depressing. It was especially depressing for me because on January 22, 1975, I would celebrate my 40th birthday. I can't say I was in a celebrating mood, but John, Lois, and Mike Riske came over for cake and ice cream. Some of my friends from home had sent me cute, humorous cards – even a few articles about life beginning at 40. But, we were still students and I couldn't believe I was 40. It seemed like just yesterday that I was 20 and in nurse's training, just before that a youngster that loved to crawl into bed with her parents. I knew I wasn't the first person to reach 40 but I disliked it. I even looked into the mirror to see if I had changed. I didn't feel older but my mirror told the truth. I was at least 15 pounds overweight and my hair was shades darker than when I was 20.

So I decided right then to buy a shampoo rinse, become a few shades lighter (I couldn't afford a beauty shop visit), I'd even try to stop eating in-between meals and cut out desserts. I knew being overweight was not only unattractive but also could be dangerous in many ways. My greatest concern was becoming diabetic if I remained overweight as both my sister and dad had diabetes. I'd try to improve my looks at 40 and not worry about numbers. I rationalized that Elvis Presley was 40 too as his birthday had been a few weeks ago. I had been a fan of his ever since I heard him as an unknown singing "Heartbreak Hotel" which had become one of his first big hits.

And I had so many wonderful memories (proving my age); of coal bins, ice delivery trucks, cars with running boards, fly paper, sky writing, war bonds, paper drives, ration books, victory gardens, air raids, "Kilroy was here", Pearl Harbor, VE Day, VJ Day, Roly Poly, Hopscotch, nickel ice cream cones, and on and on. Then a little later ballerina skirts almost to the ankle, blue jeans rolled up to the knee, ponytails and bobby sox with saddle shoes.

Yes, I knew I was 40 – it was just hard to say it.

OUR LOOSE FURNITURE

WHEN WE MOVED into our house in Springfield I was thrilled because there was a big kitchen. Now we could finally use our old round wooden table. It had belonged to Dan's parents. He had taken it from their basement when we were first married, sanded and refinished it. We had used it in Wisconsin for two years but after that it sat in the basement almost all the while we lived in Riverdale.

But now we could use it. All we needed were several wooden chairs to go with it.

When I had left the clinic in Blue Island, Illinois, all the nurses and office girls had together presented me with a 50-dollar bill. I would use that to buy four or five old chairs – I thought.

We hunted all over the city for months and found no chairs. We had a Salvation Army and Goodwill within several blocks of us so we'd look there every few weeks. We'd rummage, especially in the back room of the stores where most of the items were really junk, hoping to find something of value. Dan found an old black wooden chair. It was sturdy and strong but it was the only one of its kind.

We finally realized there weren't four chairs alike to be had in that town. The man at the Salvation Army Store told us, "When we find that many chairs alike, we repair them and put them on sale with a matching table." So we continued to use our dining room chairs in the kitchen with our round wooden table.

Then one day my sister called and said she just remembered she had three chairs in her basement that I could have. She added they were matching but needed some repair. I didn't care as long as they were made of wood.

Within a few weeks, I had all three chairs, sanded, varnished and glued. I even picked up a 4th chair at Goodwill. This chair was similar and I had refurbished it too. So, for about two weeks, we all got to sit on our new (old) chairs. Then one by one they began to come apart. I re-glued them constantly and even applied pressure with pencil and string tourniquets while they dried.

As I write this, we're on vicarage (I'm getting ahead of myself) and we're again using dining room chairs (some of them are loose too). My redone chairs sit in Dan's study waiting for him to repair them again.

Now I know and tell myself material things aren't important, but I sure wish we could sit down to a meal without a chair breaking or popping loose under us.

My front room tables are loose and wobbly and Dan says glue over glue doesn't work. So there's another reason I am getting anxious to finish, maybe then we can afford to buy four new wooden chairs.

OTHER USES FOR THE OUTLET STORES

WE USED THE Salvation Army and Goodwill Stores for other things besides old chairs. I went wild over all the old books and Dan was even able to buy himself some shoes and pants. Oh how our *Marshall Field tastes were put aside.

Every few months we were given canned goods (one can per family member) if we would all go stand in line and wait our turn. We never missed a chance to go to the food bank as every little item helped.

For a while, when we first lived in Springfield, The National Food Store provided the students with free day-old bakery goods. So, once a week we could pick up our goodies at a particular student's home. We were disappointed when this service was discontinued. But I did manage to find a discount bakery as it took a lot of bread, rolls and coffee cakes to keep a growing Mike filled.

So the Lord was always providing.

*Marshall Field – Exclusive, expensive department store located in Illinois and Wisconsin, etc.

VICARAGE ASSIGNMENT

ON MARCH 15, 1975, in a church service, Dan along with all his fellow classmates was given his vicarage assignment for the coming September. Dan Kacer – St. Matthews, Lake Zurich, Illinois was called out as Dan approached the front of the seminary gym where the services were being held. I groaned, I had never heard of Lake Zurich and I wanted to be closer to home. Dr. Niemueller would not have been proud of me.

As we later learned, Lake Zurich is located 35 miles from Chicago (the loop) and 70 miles from Riverdale. Our good friends Wally and Zelda Bochmann from Riverdale, who were with us at the ceremony, assured us that Lake Zurich was a lovely area as they had an aunt living in a nearby town.

Then, during Easter vacation, while visiting in Dolton, we took a ride with my parents to Lake Zurich. Wally and Zelda were right; the area was beautiful. The church, school, and pastor's home were all located alone on a corner about two miles outside of town. The population sign read 6,700 but we were told there were approximately 10,000 people now living in this small town situated on a chain of lakes.

We found the town to be charming with most of the business establishments fashioned after structures in Lake Zurich, Switzerland. The lake was found in the middle of town and we were not surprised that this area attracted tourists during the summer.

We were greeted by Pastor Krueger and his wife Ruth, and were shown through the church and school. We would be back in five months to start vicarage.

F R I E N D S   I N
S P R I N G F I E L D

THE CHILDREN HAD made friends and seemed to have adjusted very well at Trinity. Mike loved all sports and had several new boy friends as well as a girlfriend.

As for Yvonne, she was still going to overnights or having someone stay at our house. Her best friend was Julie Bull and Dan and I soon became friends with her parents, Red and Helen. Also, her brother Joe was Mike's classmate. They lived right outside of town and kept rabbits, a few cats and a dog. I always loved the view from their back yard as you could see the Capital and Forum 30 (Ramada Inn) was in the distance. Mike and Yvonne always enjoyed playing at their house as they have such wide-open spaces.

Then, in May, right before we were to leave, the Bulls gave a farewell pizza party for us. We had fun with Red's brother's family and the Sturms (another classmate of Mike's) were there too. They also were all members of Trinity Lutheran Church and we were sad to be leaving them. This party was the beginning of many farewells.

At the end of March Dan had started to think about taking a summer vicarage assignment. He couldn't afford to go to summer school sessions and a summer assignment would give him valuable experience before his year of vicarage began.

Now, before going any further, let me give you the definition of a vicar. In Webster's Dictionary we find: a vicar in a general sense is a person deputed or authorized to perform the function of another, a substitute in office.

In the case of the Missouri Synod Lutheran Church, a vicar is a student in the seminary. He's usually in his third seminary year and is sent to a church to assist and learn from the minister (Bishop).

I guess you could say on the Sunday he preaches he is a substitute in office. Also he helps with the order of service (liturgy), makes sick calls and helps with the various organizations within the church. The vicarage usually lasts a year but sometimes it runs for 15 months. So Dan kept correcting me when I said we had a 2-month summer vicarage. "It's a summer assignment for two months," he'd say. "Vicarage will be in Lake Zurich for a year."

In April I began to pack boxes again and lined them up in the dining room. Hadn't I just done these 10 months ago? Dan was busy preparing for finals and also was getting ready for his first (and only) sermon to be preached at Trinity. This was to be on May 4th so every time I asked him to do something he'd say, "Wait until after May 4th."

Dan was to preach at the 10:45 a.m. service and I was very nervous as usual. So were the children as they weren't used to dad preaching in front of all their friends. Also in the congregation were many of Dan's professors and classmates. But he did so well and seemed so natural I soon began to relax.

After the service we took a picnic lunch to New Salem State Park where we could just sit in a beautiful, relaxing area and unwind. The children ran the trails when lunch was over and Dan and I sat and talked. We laughed over some of the things that had happened with the children while we were in Springfield. Like the time Dan and the three children were playing checkers. While sitting on the floor, Dan was helping 3-year-old Erika play and at one point he told her, "You can jump me now." She looked puzzled, got up and walked around the checkerboard and proceeded to jump over her dad who was now stretched out on the floor. We couldn't stop laughing. Another time we went out trusting Mike and Yvonne to baby sit. They were told to potty Erika before they went to bed, which they did. But later we heard that she went to sleep while sitting on the toilet. Instead of holding her up they both watched her fall and hit her head against the bathtub. They told us weeks later. What babysitters they were – luckily she was ok – we think. Our last laughing recollection - the five of us huddled on two beanbags (the rage then) laughing for an hour as we watched "All in the Family" followed by the "Jefferson's." This occurred every Saturday night. What togetherness!

It was a warm lovely day and we loved being out in the woods. Dan was over one big hurdle and in just three weeks we'd be leaving Springfield. Little did we know it would be for good!

H O U S I N G

AT FIRST, WE planned to sub-lease our house when we left town, that is, get another sem family to live in it while we were gone (as John and Lois had done). Then, we'd have it again in our 4th year. But in April we were fortunate enough to get a sem house for our last year. Our good friends the Cooleys were living in it now and would be moving out of it when we came back from vicarage.

It was an old house located two blocks from the sem. It had four bedrooms, a big kitchen, front and dining room, but to our dismay it had no fireplace. Yet we couldn't complain, as it was only 65 dollars a month. We left our dining room hutch, our porch swing and boxes of books at our house to be (we thought).

FLOODING

FIVE DAYS BEFORE we moved we had a big rainstorm. Our dining room floor was now completely filled with boxes and we had even cleaned the shelves in the basement, as the floor down there was full of boxes too. The couple who were to move into the house had very little furniture of their own, so one of Dan's classmates brought some of his to the house for them to use while he was on vicarage. Also in the basement sat a bedroom set, a stove, a mattress and our air conditioner along with some boxes and an old trunk of Dan's.

Thus, came the big storm and how it rained. There were many black clouds, tornado warnings and all that kind of weather that comes to the Midwest in the spring.

When it was over I was talking to Lois on the phone and she asked, "How is your basement?" She had remembered how their basement had flooded two years ago right before they left for vicarage – and the storms had been similar.

Dan and I ran downstairs to find at least 6" of dirty sewage water that had backed up on the floor. John came right over. He and Dan got our air conditioner and the mattress out of the water. We really couldn't do anything about the furniture but wait until the water went down and hope it wasn't ruined too much.

Twenty-four hours later we were able to start cleaning up. What a mess. The water was gone but it had left a dirty film over everything. Mike and Yvonne were in school as Dan and I tackled the job with Erika at my side helping too. Dan's old trunk, which was at least 25 years old, was sitting in the middle of the basement and was full of wet old books, photographs, letters and some Halloween decorations. He could salvage very little of this and what he saved would smell like mildew forever. We sadly carried the trunk out to the alley to junk it.

I had kept a large cardboard box, full of rags, on the floor. I could see everything was soaked through so I picked up the whole box to throw it away. I caught a glimpse of something big, flat and black under the box and with another glance I found it to be a dead sewer rat. I screamed, dropped the box, and Dan, who was in another part of the basement, ran to me. He was actually mad at me for screaming over "such a little thing." "I have enough to do upstairs," I yelled. "I quit down here. Let Mike who loves rats, mice and things of that sort help you when he gets home," I continued as I raced up the stairs.

ANOTHER MOVE

ON THURSDAY NIGHT May 28th, the Riske's large moving truck slowly pulled away from their (John and Lois and little Mike's) house, as they stood on our front porch bidding us farewell. John had a call to Hale, Michigan, a small town of 400, along with another parish in Glennie, population 50.

John, Lois and little Mike had been eating with us for the past few days as we shared each other's food. Their refrigerator and stove had been turned off before ours so they brought their food to us. Now they were leaving for good and we would be on our way to Dolton the next day. After a few tears they were gone and we had promised to visit them soon.

My parents had arrived right before John and Lois left. They were to help us move again. On Friday, with the help of three other students, we were loaded and ready to leave within five hours. So, about 2 p.m. a caravan of two cars and a U-haul truck battled another heavy rainfall as we moved back to Dolton. We were leaving all our furniture in my mom and dad's basement and garage for the summer while we were in Minnesota on assignment.

I really want to forget all about moving but one thing my mother said, as our friends and Dan's brother helped us at the Dolton end, stands out. She turned to me as the men carried my heavy Wurlitzer organ into the basement and said, "This is a good way to lose friends, Barbara." I had no reply.

S U M M E R   I N
M I N N E S O T A

ON JUNE 10TH, we left for Eden Valley Minnesota, in my father's van. We were to be there by June 15th. Dan was to preach that day so we gave ourselves a few extra days. Mike stayed behind with gram and gramps so he could play one last year of Little League Baseball. Dan had just had oral surgery (several teeth pulled) and he didn't feel very good; otherwise, the trip was uneventful.

Before we arrive let me fill you in on Eden Valley, Cold Spring and Richmond, Minnesota. As I mentioned we were headed for Eden Valley because this is where Pastor Ron Mahnke lived. It was a town, as we were to find out, of 800 but was surrounded by many farms and seemed much larger.

Pastor, his wife Barbara and their two children Brad, 6 and Dara, 3, lived in the parsonage right next to the old deserted church. This old building had been empty for about three years and to Barbara's dismay was full of bats.

The new church was located on a hill right outside of town. It was a plain, practical church from the outside built by the hard work of the congregation which numbered about 200 communicants. The inside was beautiful as well as practical and was quite large. Upstairs, besides the church proper, was a good sized narthex and even an office for the pastor (which he didn't use because he had one at home). Downstairs was the Sunday School and Meeting Hall combined and off this was a large kitchen.

When Pastor Mahnke had taken the call to Minnesota, several years before, it was to two churches, Eden Valley's St. Paul and Cold Springs' Gloria Dei that were located 17 miles away from each other.

Cold Spring, population 2000, was the larger of the towns but their church and congregation were newer and smaller. This was the town with which we were to become most familiar. The church was located in town but still surrounded by open fields and was a mission church built by the district. The congregation had about 100 people and they would soon celebrate their 10th anniversary.

The outside of the church was beautiful. A high, A-frame type roof graced half the church and the entire building was complemented with ornate brick and large wood beams. A tall rugged cross was next to the church.

But, although the inside of the church was lovely, it wasn't very practical. The altar and several pews filled half of the church and was broken off by a cry room and organ area. Behind this was a large open room used for Sunday School, meetings, etc. A Pullman kitchen filled half of one wall; off this room were two small hallways – one leading to the restrooms and the other to the church office, where Dan was located for the summer.

As I describe this church in detail you can see I grew to love it. But, what happens as the church grows I wondered. More pews would fill the Sunday School area.

The third town I mentioned is Richmond, another small town of 800, because this is where we lived all summer. It consisted of a residential and resort area. We lived in the latter where there were mostly summer cottages, but there were a few year-round houses scattered about. Richmond was conveniently located somewhere between Eden Valley and Cold Spring. The nearest town was St. Cloud (population 45,000) located 18 miles away.

Thus, we arrived at the Mahnke's on Thursday June 12th, about 1 p.m. Mrs. Mahnke (Barbara) had a nice lunch waiting for us and a little later we went to St. Paul's to meet the pastor. Of course by then we were anxious to get settled so after a quick tour of the church (we went to Cold Spring later) they took us to our summer home which turned out to be a red cabin on a hill overlooking a lake.

Waiting there to greet us were our next-door neighbors and owners of this cabin, George and Amanda Voss. They lived in their home year-round. On the hill there were three summer cabins and two year-round houses. The inside of the cabin was ideal, small yet containing everything we needed. It had two bedrooms, a kitchen and a small parlor (which at one time had been the front porch) full of windows and off this the bath.

We even had a shower stall, which was in the parlor. Looking out the back window (in the parlor) you could see a driveway coming from a garage under our cabin and meeting a grassy stretch until it ended at Horseshoe Lake.

Here, the Vosses had their own pier and pontoon and we were to find out that Amanda was the fisherman in the family. George and Amanda were retired farmers from Bertha, Minnesota. They still kept a large garden at water's edge. They were the parents of three married children.

Within the next few days we already had a routine. Although it was cold and wet the first few weeks we were there, the girls began to fish with Amanda every evening at 7 p.m. George would work in his garden; the girls and Amanda would fish off the pier or from the pontoon, while Dan, Tuffy and I would watch.

As the summer progressed the girls were almost addicted to the sport of fishing and would call for and pester Amanda to fish even when she wasn't in the mood. Vonnie's big thrill came when she finally (at the end of the summer) put a practically dead worm on a hook but she never could take the fish off the hook by herself. Even Erika caught sunnies and once a large bullhead. Amanda would call to George, "We've got fish to clean" if the catch was large enough. Then George would cut the head off, Amanda would clean and freeze it. If they only caught a few small ones she'd throw them back or give them to the lady in the trailer across the road for her cat. I think Vonnie (like me) was always glad when we could throw the fish back. As much as she loved fishing I know she always felt sorry for the fish.

The girls also loved to help the Vosses in their garden. Early each morning they'd be outside helping with the strawberry picking. After we had been there about three weeks the strawberry season was over for a while so they began to help with the green beans. I was never surprised, no matter what time of day, to see the girls and Amanda sitting on her porch snapping beans or just visiting. They were like three girlfriends. Actually, we all began to look to the Vosses as our second parents and we would eat meals together, visit with one another and of course we'd go to church together.

Now back to that first day. It took me just a few hours to get settled in my little cabin, as all we brought with us were our clothes, sheets, blankets and our TV set. The girls and I spent the next few days exploring the area, as we walked Tuffy and Dan began preparing his sermon for his first Sunday at Gloria Dei in Cold Spring.

In front of the cabin was a grassy area, and then came the road leading to all the dwellings on the hill. Across the road lived the Lee's who lived there year-round (like the Vosses). Mrs. Lee came over one morning carrying a plate of homemade doughnuts and brought her granddaughter to play with Vonnie.

We were living on a chain of lakes as another lake bordered the highway in front of the cabin. Because we had no yard we were always on the lookout for turtles, as we'd walk Tuffy morning, noon and night. The turtles would cross the road from one lake to another and many times didn't make it to the other side. By the end of the summer, we even were used to dead turtles.

Right outside town we had spotted a restaurant called "The Blue Heron" and felt the name was quite appropriate as every day we'd see several herons overhead flying around looking for food. They'd usually stay right above the water and when they'd land, they would stand in one spot on the shore for hours at a time.

The weeks passed swiftly as Dan rotated his preaching, one week at Cold Spring and the next at Eden Valley. Then for two weeks, when Pastor Mahnke was on vacation, he had both services. What a rush. Right after the service without shaking hands with anyone, Dan would rush out to the van where we'd met him. He'd drop us off at our cabin and go on to the next church, arriving just in time for the opening, as the churches were 15 minutes apart.

THE PEOPLE

WE MET SO many wonderful people at both congregations; I couldn't even begin to mention all of them. However, I will refer to some of them. Several families invited us to their home for meals while a few took us out to eat. And still others gave us gifts of vegetables, meat and fruit. They really made us feel wanted and needed.

One of the couples from the Cold Spring congregation invited the Vosses and our family over to their house for dinner. This couple had two children and lived on a farm with chickens, cattle, pigs and geese. My girls were in their glory. We had a delicious meal of garden potatoes, fried chicken and all that goes with it. Now, I'm not much of a chicken lover (to eat that is) but I enjoyed the meal until our hostess stated, "I butchered these chickens just this morning." Why this surprised me I do not know; I really didn't expect that she would buy them from the store because they raised chickens. But it was too personal; I immediately lost my appetite and felt all my city breeding surfacing.

I kept telling Dan I felt like I was on a two-month vacation but I know it was different for him. He was preaching every Sunday, making sick and evangelism calls and attending church meetings. I could tell he loved every minute of it and he made the comment he was learning at the same time. Dan had no problem when it came to preaching; in fact I felt he was a little too strong and dramatic, at times, in his delivery. But everyone seemed to enjoy his sermons – who was I to criticize?

My average day (except for Sunday) went something like this. We'd sleep until 9, blaming it on the country air. The girls, many mornings, were up and out helping in the garden before we were awake. Then after getting Dan his breakfast and off to his office in Cold Spring, the girls and I would have a leisurely breakfast. We would then take Tuffy for a walk (unless the girls were busy with the Vosses). Usually we would walk for several blocks and look for beer cans (for Mike) along the way. When it warmed up I'd sit out in front in a lawn chair or on a blanket and read, dream or just stare at the water. How good it felt to be lazy again. The girls would be in and out of the cabin with me or with the Vosses; they didn't know how to be lazy. After lunch we would watch TV and never fought over channels, as we could only get one.

Sometimes, in place of TV, if Dan were home with the van we'd take the girls to the beach a couple miles away. At night, Vonnie and Erika would go fishing with Amanda and Dan and I would watch TV unless he had a meeting. Once or twice we even went out in the pontoon so they could fish but Amanda decided she had better luck right off the pier.

By ten o'clock I would be ready for bed. What had I done to be so tired, I'd wonder?

Monday was Dan's day off. One week, at the pastor's suggestion, he also took Tuesday off. We went further north into Minnesota to Itasca State Park. This is where the Mississippi River begins as it flows out of Lake Itasca. What a beautiful sight it was and at its origin, only a mere 10 feet wide.

CABIN
LIVING

ONE OF THE disadvantages we had was having no washing machine but this gave us the opportunity to visit Cold Spring at least twice a week. Dan would drop us off at the laundromat when he went to church. As we waited for the clothes to wash I would catch up on my reading or we would walk a few blocks to the main street and shop. When it was really hot it just felt good to stay in the air conditioning.

Most everyone knows what living in a summer cottage is like. The water was hard (was it my imagination or did the coffee taste funny?) and we had all sorts of bugs. Now I'm not complaining as we had hot water, TV, electricity, and all the comforts we needed but it still wasn't quite like home. One morning I noticed a strange looking bug crawling along the floor. It was fat, light brown and shiny. I picked it up and threw it outside. To my amazement, it bounced. Later in the day I mentioned this strange bug to Amanda who laughed and told me, "Why that sounds like a tick full of blood. Quick, look in your dog's ears."

Dan examined Tuffy and he indeed did have several ticks in both ears. From then on we knew what ticks were. Erika came into the cabin one day crying with one on her arm and I woke up in the middle of the night because I felt one crawling up my leg. We'd remove them with rubbing alcohol, fire or a hot needle as they plant themselves right into your skin.

ANOTHER
BIG MOVE

IN JULY DAN tried to get up to date with Anaheim (California) Lutheran Convention by reading the newspaper. He'd report anything of interest to me. Then one day he shocked me by saying, "The convention presented and passed a resolution for the Springfield Seminary to be moved to Fort Wayne, Indiana." Now, we had heard rumors of this nature before we left Springfield, but no one seriously thought the move would come about. Everyone figured the church was too busy with its synod problems to bother with a small matter like this.

Dan and I discussed the move. From what we could figure out we didn't think the move would concern us. The paper reports left us thinking we'd be the last graduating class in Springfield. But by the time we were to leave Minnesota we knew we'd be the first class to graduate from Fort Wayne. Our 65-dollar a month house was just too good to be true. We'd have to start house hunting, looking for new schools for the kids in a town – a place to which I had never been.

But I had plenty of time to worry about living in Fort Wayne; a more immediate concern was where we were going to live when we arrived in Lake Zurich. Dan was keeping in touch with Pastor Krueger from St. Matthews during the summer, but even when it was time to leave our summer home we still had no plans for housing in Lake Zurich.

COMPANY

OF COURSE WE had lots of company in Richmond. Dan's sister, Anne, had surprised us with a 4-hour visit with a friend just a week after we arrived. Then on the Fourth of July we were given another surprise when our friends, the Bulls from Springfield, pulled up to our front door. They came at such a good time because I had been very low and depressed that day. We hadn't seen a parade, which always had been a custom in the past. There wouldn't be any fireworks that night in the small town of Richmond. So it just didn't seem like the fourth of July to me. I guess I was homesick too, for which home I did not know. So, when Helen, Red, Joe and Julie arrived I was thrilled. The grill was going and they soon joined the Vosses and Kacers for a cookout.

Julie stayed with us for the next two days while the rest of the family found lodging in a nearby motel. We showed them the church in Eden Valley and the one in Cold Spring. We went swimming at the beach and the children fished. Then after church on Sunday, they got to hear Dan preach a second time, then headed for home.

As much fun as we were having in Minnesota, we all, as a family, missed Mike. I don't know if the feeling was mutual though as he was having too much fun at his grandparent's house with baseball and all his old friends.

We were really looking forward to the third weekend of July when my parents would be coming to Richmond with Mike in their new Champion Motor Home. Our beer can collection for Mike grew – the day came closer for the visit. When it finally came we practically ran down the highway to meet them.

It was good to see my parents relax and enjoy the beauty of this area, as they sat out in front of the cabin. Dan and I didn't relax though as we were busy taking the kids swimming and then while Dan attempted to get some work done the kids and I hiked a good deal, taking turns with Erika on our back. Mike even managed to find a few more beer cans. They had to leave all too soon but then we had to start preparing for our two-day camping trip with the Walther League. And right after returning from this trip, my sister, Carol, and her youngest daughter would be coming for a weeklong visit.

CAMPING OUT

THERE WERE ABOUT 7 youths going camping with us from our two churches, but we were getting together with several other churches too. There were two pastors in attendance and Dan, of course, the only vicar. We lived in a tent, set between the Mississippi and Pratt Rivers. It was a lovely spot but I didn't enjoy the outhouses and the only running water available was the coldwater faucet along the road. To make it worse I had only brought an electric coffee pot with us and we had no hook-up for electricity. No one else had just a regular coffee pot with them; Dan & I seemed to be the only real coffee drinkers there. So the first afternoon there, Dan and Vonnie, with most of the other kids, traveled down the Pratt River on inner tubes (it took 2-1/2 hours). Meanwhile Erika and I went out looking for a plain coffee pot. All the towns close by were very small (about 200) but finally in Rice, Minnesota, I did manage to find what I needed. It was only a 2-cup pot and cost three dollars – what expensive coffee. We would brew the coffee on the grill so it seemed to take forever, but eventually we got smart and just kept the pot on all the time. It was amazing how many people suddenly liked a cup of brewed coffee when it was available.

We fought mosquitoes off constantly (the next month there was a mosquito virus scare). But to more than make up for the hardship we sang with kids around the campfire, cooked our meals over the open fire, prayed, and took communion together that last morning.

We went home (to Richmond) tired, dirty, full of bites but we had fun we told ourselves, and do you know our cabin looked like a palace when we returned. We could go to the bathroom in comfort, take a shower with warm water and brew a cup of coffee in minutes. What luxury?

CAROL AND AMY

MY SISTER CAROL and my niece Amy, who is 8 months younger than Yvonne, were to fly from Peoria, Illinois, to St. Paul, Minnesota Airport where we'd pick them up on Monday July 30th. They were to stay a week, then fly home taking Vonnie with them. We had only 10 days left of our assignment so Erika couldn't get too bored or lonesome for her sister.

Carol and my brother-in-law Harry have three older daughters in Havana; Karen is married with a 2-year old boy named Jay Jay, Jan was married that previous October to Jerry and Nancy is attending college in Charleston, Illinois.

They had a good trip coming in and Amy was thrilled with her first flight. Actually, it was like Carol's first time flying too as the only other time was when we as children (Carol was 14 and I was 11) had flown in a small private plane for about ½ hour.

After leaving the airport we looked over the big twin cities. We saw tall buildings and busy expressways just like in Chicago. We visited Mini Ha Ha Falls in a park and took some pictures. We were then off for our cabin. My sister and I spent most of the week talking (we had to catch up on everything) as we hadn't seen each other for about three months. At the same time we took the girls swimming, went in the water, talked about everything without difficulty, went fishing out of the pontoon, shopping and touring.

We had several cookouts with the Vosses and went out to eat in the big town of St. Cloud. It was here we found an old bookstore. Because we all loved to read books of any description, Carol and I were silent for a few minutes as we searched the shelves. We then found the week slipping away

65

and before we knew it, it was Saturday. All week we had slept comfortably as Carol shared a bed with Erika and the older girls slept in sleeping bags on the floor of our parlor.

Then, Saturday afternoon we had another surprise in the person of Dan's brother Mike and our two nephews, Kevin and Greg. They had slipped away from their own summer cottage in Chetak, Wisconsin, leaving their mom and another couple behind. At that point, I rather wished I had been left behind too.

Surprisingly, I loved all the company even if it was slightly crowded. Mike and the boys stayed overnight and the girls moved their sleeping bags in with Carol and Erika. Then Mike could have the couch and the boys on the floor.

But that wasn't all of our company on that Saturday afternoon. Earlier in the week I had written to my cousin Charlotte's daughter Susan, who lived in Plymouth, Minnesota, which is 50 miles away. I explained that Carol was in Minnesota for a week and invited Susan over for supper on Saturday. I hadn't asked her to respond so I didn't know for sure if she was coming, but I wasn't surprised to see her and her roommate drive up. What a nice reunion.

After eating and a lot of visiting we all went for a refreshing ride in the pontoon. The boat sank a little deeper into the water and didn't travel quite as fast as usual but that didn't dampen our fun. Sue and her friend Irene went home later that evening. Mike and the boys left Sunday after church.

Then on Monday we took Carol, Amy and Vonnie to the airport. I was a little sad and also frightened as the jet took off with my little girl flying for the first time. At that time, I had never been in a jet myself.

Dan, Seminary Years 1973-1977

Irene, Betty in wheelchairs – Beatsie on ground, circa 1950, at
Palmer Park – Chicago

Summer of 1974 –
As we joined dad at the Seminary in Springfield, Ill

Dan, Barb, Mike, Von and Erika ready for Gram,
Gramp Kacer's anniversary Oct 1973

Dan's parents 50th wedding anniversary,
October 1973, Whiting, IN.

Circa 1973, Dolton, Ill. Helen and LeRoy Lindstrom,
Barbara's parents

Mike poses in our home, Springfield, 1974

The back of our red cottage
for the summer of 1975, Richmond, Minnesota

Camping – Summer 1975, our home for a weekend, Minnesota

Some of our many cats
while on vicarage in Wauconda, Ill., Fall, 1975

Our new home (parsonage), Winter of 1978, Gar Creek, Ill.

F O U N D A
F R I E N D

I STARTED TO pack within the next few days and Dan prepared for his last sermon, which was to be given at an outdoor service at Richmond Park, followed by a potluck dinner. We said our farewells to many of our new friends at this service, as it was for both congregations.

On Wednesday evening August 13th, we went out for dinner with Barbara and Pastor Mahnke, compliments of one of the ladies from the Eden Valley Church and on Thursday morning we bid our sad farewell to George and Amanda.

We had bid our farewells to Lois and John just a few short months ago also but now that we were on our way home, we were going to visit them in their new congregation. It meant going out of our way just a bit (about 500 miles) but it was a beautiful ride through upper Wisconsin, the upper peninsula of Michigan, around the lake and over the Mackinac Bridge into Lower Michigan where we found our destination – Hale.

As we traveled through the many small towns, we noticed each church we would pass and would wonder whether it was Lutheran. In one such town, Loana, Wisconsin, right on the main road we noticed a Missouri Synod Lutheran Church. Dan slowed up so he could catch the pastor's name and when he did he came to a complete stop. The pastor was Keith Brutlag and he had just graduated from the sem with John. Dan knew him as he had been the vicar at Trinity Church when Dan did his field work there just this past year. We backed up and found the parsonage across the street from the church but were disappointed to find Keith was visiting his dual parish, which was about 30 miles away. Dan visited with his wife for a few minutes. We continued on our way thinking what a small world it is.

Before reaching Hale we rode through Glennie, the town where John's second church was located (dual parish). We almost missed the town (not really), as its population, as I mentioned earlier is only 50. The church was actually an old bank building.

In Hale we had some trouble finding the Lutheran Church because this was another small town of 400. There were several other churches but eventually we found the right one with the Riske's house next door. Little Mike seemed bigger and he was afraid of Tuffy (he had been bitten by a dog just recently). But he and Erika took right up playing where they had left off in Springfield.

While in Minnesota, I received a letter from Lois postmarked July 17th, and in it she explained all about their new church and home. Saturday (they had Saturday evening services) was John's first time to preach and 90 people were at the service. Sunday there were 120 in Hale and 20 in Glennie. The Hale church was quite nice with a stained glass window in front in the shape of a cross and a picture of Jesus. The Glennie church was small, an old bank building, but its setup was really nice for a church. Our house is nice and is right across the driveway from the church. We are in walking distance of town and there are some really nice stores.

She went on to draw me a diagram of the house while explaining all about her 3 bedrooms, front room, dining room and kitchen. She added, "P.S. We have a built-in dishwasher and dark wood kitchen cabinets. What a surprise!"

Lois wasn't very happy she told us after we arrived, that they were so close (30 feet from the highway) and also that one side of the house was all church parking lot. The other side she said belonged mostly to the next-door neighbor but I did notice they had a small fenced in yard. I guess Mike wouldn't stay in it let alone play in it. But, with all its good and bad features we could see they were happy to be settled and loved the people and the area.

We arrived there on a Friday afternoon and our two days together quickly sped by. On Saturday morning they took us swimming to their favorite beach, Sand Lake, and that evening we attended their church services and heard John preach for the first time.

On Sunday morning, right after John left for early morning services in Glennie, we headed for home, home to my parent's house in Dolton where their basement and garage were packed with our furniture and what not.

VICARAGE IN LAKE ZURICH

ON MONDAY, AUGUST 18th, we rode up to Lake Zurich, from my parent's home, and found that Pastor Krueger had just gotten a lead on a house for us. It turned out to be a large one-story remodeled house on a Black Angus farm. The farm was located two miles outside Wauconda and seven country miles from the church and school in Lake Zurich. Wauconda, it boasts Bang Lake, is 30 miles north of Chicago (the loop) and 70 miles from my parent's home in Dolton.

Within two weeks we had moved in and the children weren't too sad to miss several days of school in the process. Again they were reluctant to make new friends, but after a few days they were adjusting. Dan took them to school each day as he went to his office at the church. In the meantime, Erika and I were busy getting the house in order.

When we were first shown this big farmhouse we believed it was more than sufficient. It had 4 bedrooms, a family room, front and dining room and two bathrooms. And to top it all off, it had two fireplaces; one in the parlor and one in my favorite room, the kitchen. When Dan and I first saw the fireplace, we laughed because we had a thing about them. Our house in Riverdale had one (part of the reason we bought it) and we were also fortunate enough to have had one in Springfield. So, as the congregation had looked for a house for us all summer, I said to Dan, "Of course, it must have a fireplace!" I wasn't really serious but here we had two of them.

The kitchen overlooked the farm, the cows, the barns, the cats and the hills. It was beautiful. Also, we had a front yard about a block long, sloping right down to the highway. It was covered with 20 old trees so we had our own park. Later I realized that my cousin Kathy Peterson and her husband Roger lived close by in Wheeling, Illinois and Erika and I were able to visit her. She fixed us a nice lunch and it felt good to get away from the farm for the day.

O U R   C A T S

THE FARM ALSO came equipped with cats and I do mean a lot of them. As we were first shown the house, my mom (who was with us) had commented about all the cats. "You'll have to get rid of some of them because of your big dog," she told us. Because of Tuffy, I agreed at the time, but after we moved in, I knew they weren't ours to get rid of. They all (20) belonged on the farm and we grew to know and love almost every one of them.

At first we had several kittens but eventually all but one died or disappeared. We think a tomcat killed one because it had no mother. It had been dumped off on the farm with another kitten that died right before we came. Then, because we had a few mice in the house (I found mouse droppings in the bread box) Dan bought some De-Con and put it in our basement crawl space. But to our dismay the day after De-Con was put out two more kittens were dead. Whether it was from De-Con or not didn't make a difference, we were heartbroken. One small, black full-grown female that always hung around the house was promptly named Blackie. We were so clever because we named a white kitten, whom we at first thought was Blackie's baby, Whitey. Whitey was the only kitten to survive that fall and we all loved to hold and spoil her.

We decided a big yellow male who was always with Blackie and Whitey looked just like television's Morris so Morris it was. Another male similar to Morris was Morris' brother and a big white and yellow male that was frequently mean to some of the other cats was called Meaney. Original? He disappeared just before Christmas.

Our friendliest cat was a cute, rather fat, female with a masked face. She seemed especially fond of Vonnie so she became Vonnie's Girlfriend.

Her look-alike was named Vonnie's Girlfriend's Sister but because this was such a mouthful to say we eventually took Vonnie off both names.

Then there was Mangy, a big yellow Persian male with shaggy matted fur. You never could tell what you might find hanging from or, in the winter, frozen to him. He walked with such a sway we wondered about him, until the lady that lived in the small cottage behind us told us he had been injured and was like a crippled person would be. Nevertheless, he was tough and chased all the strange male cats out of his domain. He was Dan's favorite but certainly not Tuffy's, as they had tangled several times. Tuffy could catch him as Mangy couldn't climb a tree, but usually Tuffy got the worst end of the deal with a bloody nose.

And, we had a Mama Cat whom we were told was at least 10 years old and probably the mother of many of our grown cats. She had two kittens in October and the kids found them in the barn when they were about 4-weeks old. Then, all of a sudden, they were moved from that spot and we thought we would never see them again. But one cold Sunday in March (five months later) I saw a small red animal slinking across the barnyard. At first, I thought it was a fox. The kids went out to investigate and found it to be a skinny, half grown cat, whose fur was dirty and covered with hay and burrs. She was friendly but frightened and seemed unfamiliar with outside surroundings. Could she be one of those kittens? Had she lived in the barn all winter and what had she eaten? Where were her brothers and sisters? We knew we would never have the answers but we immediately loved her and named her Red Fox (clever?).

Also, back in October, someone had dumped off a full-grown gray female cat at the farm. She cried and seemed to want to come into the house with us. At first she couldn't even walk and kept rubbing against Mike's leg, at the same time her front legs would give out. She didn't seem to be afraid of Tuffy but didn't like the other cats. We racked our brains and came up with the name of New Kitty for her. We think she was happy with us but we had her for such a short time. She was never really well and Mike found her dead on Christmas Eve.

Several of the farm cats were too wild or frightened to come near us and a few, although full grown, were tiny and fragile. The lady in the cottage behind us took these few cats into her house at night and eventually she was taking Red Fox inside also. We were happy to know someone else felt like we did about animals.

Are you wondering what we fed all those felines? We never worried about having leftovers go to waste; they were divided between Tuffy and all his rivals. Also, our cats appreciated any milk and cereal left by the kids. Bread crusts or any crumbs, normally given to the birds, were gobbled up by them. My mom contributed toward their food fund but I still found myself buying boxes of cat food quite frequently. Someone had to feed them. No wonder they greeted us every time we came home from somewhere or even if we'd step out onto the porch at least six of them would run up to us. Sometimes I'd feel like the Pied Piper as a trail of cats would follow me around the yard, but I knew it wasn't me that was so popular but what I represented.

At first we were appalled when they would catch a mouse and bring it right up to the house as if to say, "See what I can do." But we were soon accustomed to it as we were living on a farm with all its tranquility, the cows, the open spaces and the smells. At the same time, Dan was growing in his role as a vicar.

He preached at least once a month at first and made shut-in and sick calls as he had in Minnesota. He attended all the meetings of the church, even the Ladies Aid and Evening Guild. He seemed happy and even gained weight, something he needed, which he blamed on all the dinners at St. Matthew's. Any excuse he'd say and St. Matthews has a meal. But he certainly wasn't complaining.

We began to make new friends within the congregation and as in Minnesota, they invited us to their home or some took us out to eat. I almost hated to make new ties as we'd only be at St. Matthews for a year but how could one avoid it?

THE
CHILDREN

THE CHILDREN PARTICIPATED in everything they could in school. Mike and Vonnie both played baseball, then basketball and Vonnie became a cheerleader. They began to make new friends and it saddened me in a way. They were happiest when busy and although they loved living on a farm, they missed having kids right next door to play with them.

Erika waited patiently every day for her big brother and sister to come home from school, as she loved playing outdoors with them. When we were alone during the day she always wanted me to play house or school with her – she needed a playmate. When she (Erika) began Sunday school, I began to help out in the nursery department. Also, I attended Dan's Bible class on Romans and went to the Ladies Aid Meeting every first Thursday of the month. Erika found a boyfriend in Steve, one of our new friend's sons. So she was always happy when we had a meeting and she and Steve could play in the nursery. I didn't realize our moving so much had affected her until one day I heard her tell one of Vonnie's friends, "We move every year." I guess it did seem that way to a four-year old. This episode reminded me of something she told my mother the previous summer, right after we left Springfield. We were at my parent's home for two weeks before leaving for Minnesota and she said, "Gram, remember when we used to have a house?" My mom had felt like crying. I think like Yvonne, Erika loved living on our (rented) farm best of all. She loved the animals and our park-like yard, although as I mentioned, she needed someone to play with her own age instead of me. In the winter, Erika enjoyed sledding down our front lawn, which was actually a small hill, while Dan, Mike and Vonnie got some use out of their skis.

Tuffy and I would watch from the window and I would tell Dan not to let our landlord, the farmer know about their winter sports or he'd charge rates besides our rent.

PASTOR AND WIFE

PASTOR AND RUTH Krueger were just a few years older than Dan and I and had a lovely family of 6 children, 3 boys and 3 girls. Their oldest daughter and 2 sons were married and the daughter's husband also was a vicar that year in Michigan. We didn't know him, as he was a student at the St. Louis Seminary. The Krueger's youngest son graduated from college that June and a daughter graduated from high school. That left the youngest girl still in high school.

Pastor was kept busy with his large congregation of 1000 communicant members and Ruth served as his part-time secretary. Dan felt privileged to serve as a vicar under Pastor Krueger (he was actually Dan's Bishop as mentioned earlier); in fact, he was the first full-time vicar St. Matthew ever had.

Now, I don't want to give the impression that our year of vicarage was all honey and roses, because when people deal with people everyone doesn't always get along. Dan had a few challenges and problems but the good so outweighed the bad they're not worth mentioning.

GRANDPA KRUEGER

WHEN WE ARRIVED in Lake Zurich, Pastor Krueger's father, Dr. Ottomar Krueger, served as his assistant. He had been at St. Matthew's with his son for the past seven years. Doctor (Grandpa) had lost his wife in 1971 and resided alone in his own home in the town of Lake Zurich. Although 83 years old, when we first met him, he was as active and alert as any man twenty years his junior.

Dan admired Dr. Krueger and felt he could learn so much from him. He had been in the ministry for 62 years. During that time he had served several congregations and taught English and History at Fort Wayne, Indiana. Also, he had served as President of the Jr. College in Fort Wayne, which was his alma mater. His last church, before coming to St. Matthew, had been Zion Lutheran in Akron, Ohio. He had been the Central District President for 12 years.

Thus, how saddened we were when this wonderful man was called home on February 19, 1976. We had only known him for six months but had grown to love him in that short time. Dan felt richer for having worked with him. And he had continued to serve his Lord in the church up until about a month before his death!

THE FAMILY

WE WEREN'T THE only ones who loved our big house and its surroundings. Dan's family loved to visit us in Wauconda. His brother Mike, wife Jan, and their two sons, Kevin and Greg, came up quite often and brought gram and gramp Kacer with them. Although Dan's parents were both approximately 82 years old, they still loved to walk around outdoors. Grampa would hobble with his cane and gram would be next to him stopping frequently to pick weeds and talk to the cats. Dan then would always scold me for being such a poor gardener.

Our sister-in-law Jan enjoyed picking dried weeds in the fall while her boys played ball with their three cousins. She would stoop down to pick a weed and ironically at the same time the farmer's big show bull would moo over the fence. So we'd all yell in sing-song fashion, "Jan's got a boyfriend."

Dan's sister Amy and her husband K. O. would come quite often too, bringing gram and gramp or Dan's other sister Anne. Tuffy would really get excited when they came because K. O. and Amy always took him for walks.

My mom and dad came to visit quite often too, especially after my dad retired in January. They had spent a few months in Florida and then came home in the spring and sold their Champion Camper. Then, in June, they sold their house and traveled between my sister's house in Havana and our place, also taking a trip to Wisconsin in between.

Eventually, they would help us move again, to Fort Wayne this time, where they'd stay with us for just a few months. Then, they'd go to Florida for another few months, followed by a short visit to California. They talked about settling in Florida when we finished our schooling. I wondered though, could they really settle anyplace? They were gypsies at heart.

The holiday season was great fun spent on our farm with even Doris and Bob Foyut, Bobby and Gail, Wally and Zelda Bochmann, and Mariann (all from Riverdale) coming to visit us.

Christmas Day on vicarage brought our families to the farm for food, fun and fellowship. Dan was unwinding again after a wonderful learning experience during the Advent Season so we all really enjoyed the day. The people from St. Matthew had been kind and generous to us during the Christmas season with gifts of food and money. Dan had said people usually love students (no matter what age) and with us they had five to love. Forgive me for bragging but they did love us five times as much; at least it felt that way to us.

TUFFY

I'VE TALKED ABOUT how Dan, the children and me had adjusted to the different areas in which we lived; now I'll explain Tuffy's situation.

I think our first move to Springfield was especially traumatic for Tuffy, as he was already seven years old and had always lived in the same house. As I told Dan and he laughed, I couldn't explain the move to Tuffy, as I could to the children.

In Riverdale, Tuffy had his own yard and he also had his yard in Springfield and this helped his confusion but he seemed out of sorts for the first several days in our new house. Dan always said as long as he's with us and has our bed (yes, he slept with us in the cool weather and under the bed in the summer) he'd be all right.

Although we had a huge fenced in yard, we still walked Tuffy because of all the cats. Mike had the job of walking him before and after school. Dan took him out at 10 pm so I was elected for the 11 am shift. Erika and I always walked him the block down our driveway to the highway. She'd run ahead and ward off the cats; they weren't afraid of any dog and I'd try to pull Tuffy toward the road. Then upon reaching the highway he'd have the nerve to bark at the cows grazing along the fence.

When we had been in Wauconda about seven months Tuffy did calm down a bit; in fact he may have become a little too familiar with the farm. It seemed every time a car, truck or motorcycle would pass on the road, which wasn't very often, Tuffy would bark at them. He wasn't used to the traffic any more – he was a country dog!

THE COWS

WE ALL LOVED being surrounded by the big Black Angus cows. I would talk to them as they stood by the fence watching us. They'd continue to chew their cud as I walked a barking Tuffy past them and sometimes they'd even tilt their heads in a questioning way.

But, several times, they gave us reason to be concerned. The first time was one cold, snowy morning in February, as we were getting ready to go to church. I spotted one out in the barnyard; he had somehow gotten away from the others. Dan and Mike ran outside and tried to coax the cow back where he belonged. I could see them through the window and could just imagine them saying, "Here cow, Here cow." In the meantime, I called the farmer. He and his daughter were there within fifteen minutes and had the cow back in where he belonged in no time.

Several cows did get out again in the months to follow, but we would just keep our eye on them so they wouldn't venture near the road to the highway. Eventually someone would get them back where they belonged. But, one morning I noticed the two youngest calves out chasing a cat (Girlfriend) right into the yard. I called the farmer, talked to his wife who assured me they'd stay near their mother who was inside the fence; and they did.

Then, one afternoon in the middle of May, as I was doing dishes, I was shocked to look out the window to see about twenty cows in the barnyard with more streaming out through the barn and some of them were really big! Dan, Mike and Vonnie ran out and tried flagging them back with a shirt while Erika watched from the yard. I kept my watch from the kitchen window but before I knew it, there came Vonnie racing toward the house with a cow at her side. I don't know who was more frightened. Erika who had ventured out was scared too and Mike was carrying her. Before the farmer arrived, my city turned farm family had corralled most of the cows back. What fun, what excitement, what could compare with this when we moved back to the city?

CLOSE TO NATURE

ONE OF THE truly beautiful things about living on a farm was being so close to nature and moving to the farm in the fall gave us a chance to see the gorgeous colors Mother Nature spread to all of the countryside. We lived a mile away from Wauconda Apple Orchard and for several Sundays we could hardly get to the highway because of all the traffic. People drove for miles to this area to pick apples and to see the rolling hills, many lakes and the colors at this time of year.

Our winter wasn't too harsh but in January we did have several inches of snow, which stayed for almost a month. Our view out the front window was breathtaking; huge pine and oak trees glimmered with snow making it a winter wonderland. Then in spring, everything, the trees, flowers and grass woke up. We were surrounded by lush green beauty although Dan and Mike didn't think it was so beautiful when they had the big lawn to mow.

With the warm weather, Dan and the children enjoyed shooting golf balls down the hill and when summer came I enjoyed sitting in my lawn chair at the top of the hill, just basking in the sun. I had time to think and reflect. I realized how fortunate I was to have my family and was thankful each day that we all remained healthy. Also, Dan and I were so blessed to each have both of our parents alive and well.

I humbly felt I grew a little stronger as a Christian during that year. I couldn't recite more Bible verses or find the books of the Bible any faster, but I could talk to God and I found I was praying more often, not just asking for things but thankful prayers.

WE MUST LEAVE

WHEN IT WAS almost time to leave Lake Zurich, I'd sit and watch the children play ball in the yard with the kittens at their heels. I would pray "Dear Lord give me the strength to be brave and not too sad when we would leave our home on this Black Angus farm. It's so beautiful here and we will never find another place quite the same. Help me in all my farewells to our friends at St. Matthews. I hate goodbyes. Thank you for all the blessings bestowed on us this past year." When I would walk Tuffy each day out onto the highway, up the hill, I would feel so close to the Lord. The sky and ground seemed to merge, the birds would be chirping and cows were a part of the landscape on the hill. I'd marvel each time and think to myself, I should take someone that doesn't know or believe in God, with me up on this hill.

CELEBRATIONS

ON FRIDAY, APRIL 9th, my sister Carol and brother-in-law Harry celebrated their 25th wedding anniversary. They were blessed with four daughters and a grandson. We had a small dinner party for them at our house in celebration of the occasion. My mom and dad were there too to join in the fun. We ate a casserole dinner and also had wine in front of a roaring fire in our kitchen fireplace. And, to top everything off, I had made Carol and Harry a scrapbook with the story of their marriage (with a few errors) and lots of photographs. After dinner the guests of honor went to the Lincolnshire Resort for the weekend where they enjoyed dining, theater and golf. As this establishment was only ten miles from our home, they left their youngest daughter Amy with us for the weekend.

On Sunday, Palm Sunday, our Mike was confirmed but Carol, Harry and Amy had to leave for home right before the service. That afternoon, the Kacers, my parents, the Bochmanns and the Foyuts helped us to celebrate.

The next day we were thrilled to have the Bulls visit us in Wauconda (they didn't surprise us this time as they had in Minnesota). They were with us for three days and then it was Easter.

EASTER
1976

EASTER MORNING, APRIL 18, 1976. What a glorious day! Dan and I were up at 4:45 and Mike just a few minutes later. It was light outside and already a temperature of 60. The farm was awake; the cats were looking for their breakfast and the cows with their calves already munching on theirs. Dan had to preach at the 6 A.M. service and Mike was to help with the breakfast immediately following the service. I drove them in to church leaving Vonnie, Erika and Jerry sleeping. Jerry is my cousin Jean's son from California who was stationed at Great Lakes Naval Base. Because this base was just a half hour from our home, we picked him up on Saturday to spend Easter with us.

Driving home from church, I felt God's presence everywhere; in the weather, with the hint of spring in the air, with the fluttering birds overhead and with the beauty of the countryside. And I heard a choir singing over the radio. I didn't know the song they were singing but the words went something like this: We talk about the weather, we talk about things that aren't too important, so we really should want to shout out and talk about something that really is, we should talk and shout telling everyone that Jesus Christ is King. How perfect and beautiful my Easter morning began and now as I write this, it is time to wake up Jerry and the girls.

Erika will run around and hunt for her basket from the Easter Bunny but even at four she knows the real meaning of Easter. I asked her yesterday to be sure and she said, "Jesus is alive again."

MORE ABOUT OUR CATS

BY THE END of March it was obvious that four of the cats were expecting little ones. We had watched the males pursue the females for the previous few months and felt the children were getting a good education. Even Erika sort of understood what was happening.

On Sunday April 21, after church, we discovered that Girlfriend had her kittens on our front, screened-in porch. We had put cardboard boxes out and she had picked one of them in which to have her four kittens. The weather had been so mild just a few days before but now it was cold and even down to freezing at night. So, we covered her box with an old wool blanket and gave Girlfriend our tender loving care.

Just five days later, as Dan and I were leaving for our circuit rally at St. Matthew's, Blackie appeared to be in labor on the side porch, which we used most frequently to enter the house. So we weren't surprised when Vonnie called us at church to say Blackie was having her kittens on the porch. When Dan and I arrived home about an hour later we found her right up against the door with two little black kittens on the cold concrete. Dan went into the house and got a box into which I put a rug and some rags. Then gently he lifted Blackie and her newborn kittens into the box. One kitten was very still and we thought it might be dead. We put the box right next to Girlfriend's and now it seemed we had a cat maternity ward. The night wasn't too cold so we put a light over the box. In the morning we found two yellow kittens added to Blackie's litter, and they were all alive.

About a week later Mama Cat came running up to me as the children left for school. I could see she had just had her kittens and needed nourishment. That evening, the children tried to follow her to the barn to find the babies but it was to no avail. They were afraid to venture in too far because of the cows and I was just as glad. We had enough cats without looking for more. Girlfriend's sister had her kittens a few days later and although she and Mama were always around to eat we never saw their kittens.

Until they were six weeks old, we had eight kittens running around underfoot. To make it worse, when they were about a month old, the porch wasn't their domain any more. They became brave and ventured all over the yard and around the house with the big cats. I was so afraid someone would step on one of them, but somehow they survived.

Girlfriend's four kittens became so fat and furry. We soon named them Mousie, Girlfriend Jr, Mini Mangy and Meaney Jr. At the same time, Blackie's kittens were so small and scrawny. This didn't mean we loved them any less. Actually we only named one of Blackie's kittens and that one was an obvious decision, and the black one looking the most like her we called Blackie Jr. We certainly had a lot of Juniors hanging around. We did have another black one (they were the oldest two, remember?) besides the two that were different shades of yellowish orange.

The Hollands, who lived on a farm and were members of St. Matthews, took the first of our kittens, Mousy and Meaney Jr. when they were just five weeks old. Then a few days later the Hadlers took one of the black kittens and the smallest light colored kitten of Blackie's. We decided to keep the other four, but without even trying, another member of the congregation wanted a kitten. So when he was 12 weeks old, Mini Mangy had a new home.

We loved all the kittens but thought Girlfriend Jr. was especially darling so Vonnie and I decided we'd take her to Fort Wayne with us. So those last few weeks before we left we had fun watching Blackie Jr, Girlfriend Jr. and the remaining light colored kitten (who Vonnie insisted on calling Peachy) playing and nursing from Blackie and Girlfriend. Now, I thought Peachy was a silly name but regardless of any of their names, all the kittens had it made as they all had two mothers.

WE LOOK FOR A HOUSE IN FORT WAYNE

IN APRIL, RIGHT after Easter, we went to Fort Wayne, Indiana, to look for housing. As usual, my parents went with us. They were selling their house and maybe would stay with us for a few months in Fort Wayne.

We didn't have much to choose from and everything, as expected, was so expensive. We actually saw just one house; it was new in fact and not quite finished. It had three bedrooms, two baths, a big kitchen, front room, a 2-car garage and a basement.

Now for the bad features; it was located behind a garage and there were old cars and parts all over the property. Also, the expressway was right behind the house so it was quite noisy and the rent was $185 per month. And to make matters worse, there was no hook-up for washing clothes as the well wasn't large enough and didn't produce enough pressure. So I would have to go to the coin wash all year, as I had for the few months in Minnesota. So, we looked at some apartments but that very day they had changed their rule – no animals. We went home discouraged but determined to return to find a suitable house for our family.

We returned to Fort Wayne on the 5th of July and combined a mini-vacation with our house hunting. Gram and Gramp Lindstrom were with us again and we had two adjoining rooms at a Howard Johnson's. As Dan made telephone calls and looked through the paper for houses the kids and I enjoyed the pool. In fact, we enjoyed it through Thursday afternoon (we had arrived on Monday night) and still hadn't found a thing. This time though we had seen the inside of several houses; two farm houses, one smelly and dirty, another not too bad but too far out of town for the money, and a third house; we fell in love with it.

It was a brick two-story located right near the seminary, but they were asking $325 a month, which we could never afford. The house was well worth the price for someone else as it had five bedrooms, a large kitchen with a front and dining room combination. Also, it had two baths, a sun porch and a fireplace in the partially finished room in the basement. My parents said, "Let's take it." They would live with us then and this house could well provide for all of us. But the owner was strict and wanted no animals. I was relieved; the price was too much especially for students. My parents were so generous; we continued to look. And look we did, at apartments; several would take dogs but only 15 pounds or under. I told Dan "Carry Tuffy in your arms and pretend he's little." Tuffy weighed over 60 pounds.

Then, late on Wednesday, we reconsidered the nice farmhouse but it was already taken. So, we stayed Thursday and looked at three more houses (to buy this time) but they were either too expensive or too small. We checked out of the motel and began to drive out of town. Then my dad said, "Why don't we stop and see Pastor Weber; he lives right outside town." We had met Pastor Weber in April and he had led us to that one house, not quite completed. A member of his congregation was building it. So we stopped to see him hoping maybe he knew of something else or just maybe that house was still available. It was a long shot but we found him home on his lunch hour and followed him to the site of the new house.

The house still wasn't quite finished but was available for $150 a month this time. The owner, Bill Mullineaux, promised he would have things finished up in a month.

The house looked beautiful to me. Also, it was brand spanking new. I didn't even mind anymore that I'd have to go out to do the laundry. We had gone in a complete circle and were back to the first house at which we had looked.

Pastor Raymond Weber served Suburban Bethlehem Lutheran Church, a medium-sized congregation right outside Fort Wayne. There was a Lutheran school next to the church, which had about 80 students. In our new home, since we lived only two miles from the congregation, the girls could go to school there and were going to be out in the country (in a sense) again minus the cats and cattle.

So we went happily back to Wauconda to enjoy five more weeks in our big, old farmhouse. We were happy to have an address to give the movers on moving day, but sad in a sense too.

T H O S E   L A S T
D A Y S   O F
F A R M   L I F E

EVERY DAY, I would say to Vonnie, as we fed the cats or just sat on the front porch, "How can we leave all this?" Yet, we were also anxious to leave and get it over with as Dan hadn't been in a classroom for 15 months and knew it wouldn't be easy to go back. I'd have to go out and find a job, which I dreaded.

I don't know where the summer had gone but Mike and Yvonne had enjoyed playing ball in Lake Zurich. They both had made the All Star team and because of their baseball, we became good friends with the Harnacks, Ron and Barbara. We already knew them from St. Matthews, but because their son Jeff played with Mike and daughter Paula with Vonnie, we found ourselves together quite often. Also, they had a son, Donald, who although he was a few years older than Erika, he always enjoyed playing with her. So, we had some good fellowship with the Harnacks and the Hadlers during the summer and when on July 11th, we had open house for the congregation (so everyone could see our lovely dwelling) Barbara Harnack and Lois Hadler were nice enough to be co-hostesses.

After the baseball seasons were over (but before Mike's All Star Game) Mike went to Springfield for five days to visit a friend. At the same time, Vonnie went with my mom and dad to Havana (my sister's home) to visit with cousin Amy Jo. By the time they came home I had packed boxes and piled them up all over the house.

Besides the cats, cattle and mice on the farm we'd see rabbits hopping across the front yard from time to time. Then one night something new was added. Erika had come running into the house to tell me to look outside. There, halfway down the sloping yard, was a skunk! Blackie and Girlfriend ran up to it and I thought here comes the stink. But instead they each came back with something in their mouth, a dead bird or a mouse or both. I think they had taken these goodies away from the skunk but I never did venture close enough to know for sure.

Vonnie and I would sit and reminisce during those last few weeks. We laughed as we remembered the time Blackie was up on the awning over the porch and it was feeding time. Mike was really concerned and was sure she couldn't get down by herself, so he climbed up on the railing and gently lifted her down. Then just the next week, we spotted her on the chimney. It was winter and she knew where it was warm. Mike refused to get her down that time.

During those last few weeks we were invited on a picnic, to several homes for dinner, and to a swimming party with dinner at Vonnie's friend's home. The grown-ups had steak while Kelly (Vonnie's friend) had invited several boys and girls over for a farewell party. They were content with hot dogs.

The Kacers came up to see us on Sunday August 8th for a last cookout and get-together on the farm. Gram and gramp Kacer watched us and laughed as we played baseball and ran three legged races. Aunt Amy, Jan and I were in tears during the races as we were so bad; the kids took all the honors in that sport.

The following Tuesday my parents came to Wauconda from Havana; they were to stay with us until we moved. Wednesday August 11th was gramp's 67th birthday, but we were again invited out for dinner and then to a farewell party for us at Pastor and Ruth's house. Dan was almost in tears at the party as the Chairman of the Board of Trustees presented him with a gold wall cross and a note stating he's be getting one hundred dollars a month for the next 9 months of school. And he did cry as he wrote the following article for the *August Voice* (the church paper).

FROM THE VICAR'S VIEW

All of us travel roads perhaps taking them for granted. As our family will once again be on the road traveling (to our church's seminary to complete our courses of study for the office of the Holy Ministry) we leave full of gratitude and thanks to the Lord Jesus Christ for all of you, His people at St. Matthews.

We would share with you the Scriptural truth; that God is with His people no matter what the road may appear to be. Consider these roads on which God has directed, protected and led His people.

The Road Out of the Garden of Eden

Adam and Eve would have stayed there in their sin; it was the only place they knew. God remembered the Tree of Life and He led them out of the Garden. "Lest they should eat of the fruit", an act of mercy, God's plan of salvation would redeem them from their sin.

The Road Out of Egypt

After the Passover night, God led Moses and his people out of slavery into freedom to serve Him, the One True God. That road included: their rescue in the Red Sea, the 40 years in the wilderness and finally the Promised Land.

The Way of the Cross

Of all the roads mentioned in Scripture, this road traveled by Jesus, our Savior, is the most precious. On this road we see the great love of God for us and know because of Jesus and His work, we are saved.

The Jericho Road

For the Vicar particularly, this road will always remind me of my Bishop, Pastor Krueger. He has been more than a Good Samaritan to my family and me. He is my professor, my counselor and a friend. Thank you Pastor Krueger.

The Damascus Road

How amazing is God's Grace and Mercy? Just read the account of St. Paul's Damascus Road experience. Though we have not had such a dramatic spectacular experience, God's Grace and Mercy has been very real among you, His people. Your love for Jesus and eagerness to share the Gospel with others makes us grateful to God for such dedicated people.

There are a few other roads of course, perhaps taken for granted by many of you. These are roads which have particular meaning to us and which we will remember for years.

Old McHenry Road – it is on this rural road that your beautiful church is located. What a wonderful center for all your parish activities.

Fairfield Road – as we drove back and forth each day on this curving and hilly road, we were reminded of the beauty, majesty and serenity of God's creation.

Midlothian Road – from Lake Zurich to Libertyville, to the hospital visits of the sick and hearing from them such beautiful testimonies of faith that I often wondered, "Did the Lord send me to comfort and strengthen or to be strengthened?"

Garland Road – those of you that were able to visit our home know why we are grateful. More than adequate, our entire family appreciated it all; the cats, mice, cattle and trees.

We know that as we leave your midst there is no possible way to adequately say "Thank You" unless it is to remind you that each of you have been part of the training of a man for the ministry of the Lord Jesus Christ.

Your work in this geographical area is not finished; my academic preparation is not finished. Therefore, we must part company and yet we are one in the Lord.

Our prayers for you and gratitude to our Heavenly Father, for each and every one of you is best summed up in these words; The Lord bless you and keep you. The Lord make His face shine upon you and be gracious unto you. The Lord lift His countenance upon you. And give you peace on the road He leads you.

THE MOVE TO FORT WAYNE

ON AUGUST 15 Dan preached his final sermon at both services. After many sad goodbyes (again), we left for Fort Wayne, Indiana. Vonnie and I didn't even look back as we left our farm and all our cats. At least we were taking Girlfriend Jr. with us.

Again we were in a caravan as we picked gram's car up in Dolton. I rode with her, Dan had Tuffy with him in the Chrysler and gramp had the kids and the kitten in his new van. The movers had come on Saturday morning (the 14th) and we were to arrive in Fort Wayne on Monday, so we stayed at a motel just a few miles from the new house Sunday evening. Our new house at 4411 Short Drive was nice but oh so small compared to what we were used to. Dan had planned to use the basement as his study but it was too damp so he took over half the kitchen which fortunately was quite large.

We just left many boxes packed as we moved in and with some furniture, piled them up in our two-car garage. We had many new things to which we had to adjust; a different house, new surroundings, we were now surrounded by old cars and parts of cars instead of Black Angus because as I mentioned earlier we lived behind a garage. We also had to get used to new sounds, noisy traffic instead of the serenity of the farm with just a few moos, because we lived right off the expressway. You could hear the big semis go by, especially at night, but after a few weeks, we barely heard a thing.

We had to find new schools, a church – I guess we had already settled on Suburban Bethlehem, grocery stores and a laundromat. And, all our TV channels were so different, only three as opposed to numerous ones in Chicago. But we were settled quickly with gram and gramp there to help and by Thursday I had all my curtains up and Dan's study in some order.

When we walked out the front door we were still out in the country, in a fashion, with only one little house across the dirt road (Short Drive). The Harts lived there, Jerry who worked for our landlord Bill at the Double B Garage and his wife Barbara. Barbara's sister Alice lived with them temporarily and had a 4-year old daughter, so Erika had a playmate for a short while.

I still walked Tuffy but how different it was. As I walked down Short Drive to the highway I passed another small house and then a house trailer. Dogs would be barking from all directions so sometimes I would just walk Tuffy around the house several times. He'd sniff at the high weeds along the expressway fence and urinate on old car motors or any other parts that happened to by lying there. I knew this area would eventually be landscaped and made pretty but we wouldn't be around long enough to appreciate it.

Oh, how I missed my hills and cows, cats and the whole farm. Then on Thursday night of that first week, when we took the girls to Suburban Bethlehem Lutheran School, we received a jolt that made me all the more homesick for Illinois. All year, I had been preparing Erika for kindergarten. At Lake Zurich we had become good friends with the kindergarten teacher, Mrs. Johnson, and I kept telling her "I wish Erika could stay and be in your class." Well, on Thursday, at registration, we found Erika couldn't go to school at all as she wasn't old enough. It seemed in Indiana you had to be five by October 1st and Erika's birthday is October 15th. In Illinois the deadline is December 1st and we had never thought of the difference in state laws. We hoped to return to Illinois (God willing) after graduation and this meant next year she'd be old enough to go to the first grade without having had kindergarten

I felt so bad for Erika (and for myself too); she was so confused. I had her school dresses all ready for the fall; the plaids, long sleeves and she even had a tote bag in which to carry all her papers. When we got home I said; "Mrs. Johnson will be sad when she hears you can't go to school." Erika replied, "let's call up and tell her" and I would have except that our phone still hadn't been connected.

In bed that night everything caught up with me. I was reading a Bible verse; one of the many Pastor Krueger had given us during evangelism briefings at St. Matthews Church. It was from Proverbs 3:5, "Trust in the

Lord with all your heart and do not rely on your own insight." Beautiful words and I did trust in the Lord but I could hear the TV blaring the music "Hail to the Chief" as President Ford was just re-nominated to run for the Republican Party and the tears began to fall. I was crying for a year that was over and would never be again. I was crying for friends, for memories, for beauty, and I was crying because I hadn't cried when we left Lake Zurich. One of my new good friends had cried and one of Vonnie's girlfriend's had been sobbing too. But I felt no emotion then; I had been too busy and excited. But now I felt it and I was also feeling sorry for myself. I was tired of always adjusting to new locations and situations. I was crying because of my little girl, Erika, who couldn't go to school as we had been planning.

We registered Mike for high school (Concordia Lutheran) and he had football practice every morning even though school wouldn't start for three weeks. As I got the house in order, I knew I had better find my role, in a job, for the following year. Our money was running low but now that Erika wasn't going to school, where, when and how would I work? I guess I was too anxious and grabbed the first job into which I looked. It was for a nursing home about four miles away from our house. I was to be oriented on days for a week and then work two nights a week, 11-7. As I filled out the application I was apprehensive; why was I doing this?

For one thing I had told Dan "I'll never go back to the hospital, it's been too long (9 years). If I can't find work at a clinic I'll work in a store or clean houses." But here I was planning to work at a nursing home, which was entirely new to me.

After my week of days I felt no better about the situation. I loved the patients and the other nurses were all so nice to me but I guess I was afraid, as it had been too long since I had done this type of work. I wasn't looking forward to nights at all and there were so many rules concerning charting because of Medicare and Medicaid. My head was swimming and I didn't relish going out at 10:30 two nights a week when the rest of the family was going to bed.

I had a week off before starting on the night shift but within a few days I had made a decision. Why should I be so miserable? What was I trying to prove? I called the Director of Nursing and regretfully gave her my resignation.

Maybe after a refresher course, at another time, in another place, I could work in a nursing home, but not now.

Monday November 1, 1976
Two months have passed since I quit my job at the nursing home and so much has happened. But I haven't been able to put anything down in

my journal (I call it this to tease the kids) because of what happened to Girlfriend Jr.

She adjusted so well to our new home and stayed outside during the day and slept in the garage at night. We were still afraid to put her inside because of Tuffy. After we had been in our home about two months, Girlfriend Jr. wouldn't eat so thinking she might have worms, we made an appointment for her and Tuffy to visit the vet. The appointments were for a Saturday morning and briefly here's what happened.

Erika was playing outdoors with a neighbor girl while she waited for us to get ready. Vonnie and I had just fed the kitten with an eyedropper and I told Von to put her outside for a few minutes. Dan went out around that same time and saw Erika playing in the car, a place she shouldn't have been, so he yelled to her, "Get out of the car and slam the door after you." She did as she was told, including slamming the door even though poor Girlfriend Jr. happened to be right in the way as she closed the car door.

I'll admit I was hysterical and that didn't help Vonnie. Erika kept saying, "I closed the door when daddy told me to but it stuck and I had to really push it hard a few times."

Heartbroken, Vonnie laid Girlfriend Jr., who was already dead, down in the high weeds, behind the house and we took Tuffy alone to the vet.

We all felt so bad, Dan too, that he asked the receptionist if she knew where we could get a new kitten. We were given an address and that afternoon went and picked out not one but two female kittens. They were house cats having been born and still living in a house with their mother and six siblings. Also living in the house was a big dog.

But, when we got them home they were afraid of their new surroundings and ran and hid under anything and everything. This made Yvonne and I even more sad and lonesome for our Girlfriend. After a few days they began to adjust and really took to Tuffy, who would just tolerate them. Why hadn't we given Girlfriend a chance with him?

By now, the kittens were getting big and sassy. One was mostly white with gray spotting and long thick fur. Although her name (registered at the vet) is Fluffy, we can't seem to call her anything but Fatty. Her sister, on the other hand, being thin and black with some white markings, is called Skinny. We named her Bandy for Bandit because she has a mask on her face. I think we've called her that twice; she's just Skinny.

They race through the house, especially at night, and are such babies about going outside. They've ruined several of my plants and I was always finding dirt on the floor so I finally moved them to another spot. But regardless of all the trouble, Fatty and Skinny are already part of our family.

Dan started back to school on September 13th and even without a job is still busy with all of his studies; he always has his nose in a book. We both had post-vicarage blues those first few weeks after coming to Fort Wayne. It seemed so strange for Dan to sit with us in church week after week as we attended Suburban Bethlehem Church.

We've become friends with Pastor Weber and his wife Lois and Mike rides to school each day with two of their sons. Dan and I are attending Bible class together, during Sunday School, and are getting to know most of the other students and their families and we've renewed our friendships with all of our classmates. We've talked over some of our vicarage experiences; yet we're all concerned with one thing; finishing up this last year. Yesterday Dan preached and conducted the services at Suburban Bethlehem, the first time since vicarage. I told him, "See, you still know how even after 2-1/2 months."

Mike loves high school, especially the sports, but we haven't seen a report card yet. He played in seven football games and although we didn't understand the game the girls and I enjoyed them along with Dan. It got quite cold outside the last few games and Erika and I ended up in the car waiting for the end.

Mike is lucky and always has money for spending, as he was fortunate enough to get a job working every Saturday morning for our landlord, Bill, in his garage. But Mike complains we again live in an area where we have very few neighbors and no other children around.

Yvonne has become a very good athlete and just finished playing out the volleyball season. Now on to basketball. Her best friend here seems to be Carla – the daughter of another sem student. Between Dan and I, we get Yvonne to and from school each day. I pick her up most of the time as Dan's classes usually run into after school hours. Lately I feel like I'm always in the car (I drive my mother's Oldsmobile this year) as I also pick Mike up from football practice every Wednesday and my new job involves a lot of running around.

My new profession is that of a house cleaner; what a switch from my nursing career at the clinic. At times I'm depressed about it but most of the time I really enjoy it. I clean six houses (I have nervous energy) so I'm busy all week starting on Tuesday through Saturday. I obtained the jobs through the seminary so the pay isn't great but it sure does help. All the houses I clean are located in the same area, about six miles from home, and I'm able to take Erika with me. She sits and watches TV while I work and sometimes even helps me. Friday is my hardest day as I do two houses and each one has three bathrooms; that means six toilets in a day. I told Dan instead of dishpan hands I have toilet hands. At least I'm not under a lot of pressure and I am making just enough to buy groceries each week. I'm also getting to know each family for whom I work, even though they usually are not home. It is easy to pick up the personality of each family member as you work in his or her home week after week.

I usually start cleaning at 8:30 and finish around noon. This gives me all my afternoons free, except on Friday, and I can go to bed at night with everyone else. Also, I don't have to find a baby sitter for Erika.

My mom wrote a few days ago; they'll be going to Florida directly from California. They are planning to rent a home in Florida but will probably be back here for Christmas.

In my leisure? I am knitting and crocheting Christmas presents and also trying to read a book a week for pleasure. I do most of my reading at bedtime. Erika and I go to the library every two weeks and she enjoys getting four or five books out to look at and for me to read to her. Yvonne and I try to read to her as much as we can. We're also playing school with her all the time. After going in front of the school board and being refused, Dan and I have accepted the fact that Erika won't be going to school this fall.

November 8

It's Monday again, my day off, and I'll try to add something to my journal at least every other week so I can keep up-to-date.

This week has been important because it was election week. Dan and I had registered to vote and went to the firehouse (our polling place) in our area about 5pm last Tuesday. We were all set to cast our votes but the line was at least an hour long, so with the girls at home alone and supper cooking on the stove, we couldn't wait. I felt a little guilty about it, especially after President Ford lost. I really didn't think Jimmy Carter could beat him. Now I think Mr. Carter must be a nice man, but I just don't feel any grown man in the limelight should be called Jimmy. But, I imagine I'll get used to it after a while.

Also, this past week, my parents called from California. They are going to Las Vegas (hard to take) for the weekend and then said they would be leaving on the 9th, tomorrow, for Florida. Christmas in Fort Wayne is also on the agenda – yeah!

Mike, to our surprise and disappointment, tried out and didn't make the freshman basketball team. He had always been such a good player in grammar school playing on the starting team but I guess the competition really gets rough in high school. Mike confessed he wasn't doing his best at practice but he went on to say, "I'd rather be good and make it next year when we're settled in one place." I can see he is getting anxious to finish up here too.

This morning it was especially hard to get up. I never set an alarm but just my mind to the time. This a.m. my mental alarm got me up late. I did wake up at 6:45 and thinking I had 15 minutes I went back to sleep until 7:15. Guess I better start using the clock now that winter is approaching and it is getting darker in the morning. We were all up late last night watching "Gone with the Wind" Part I, which was on TV for the first time. Of course the children had never seen it so it was fun watching it together.

When I looked outside this morning there was at least 1-1/4" of snow on the ground; a little early this year but that didn't even lift my spirits (I love snow). This morning when I looked into the mirror on my dressing table I didn't like what I saw. I had crows feet on both sides of my mouth; that hormone cream wasn't working and my hair was ugly and getting dark again. When we left Riverdale in 1974 I left behind my fancy hairstyles. My beautician was also my best friend Doris and I could always count on her for a haircut, frosting or fancy hairstyle.

Before we moved I asked her, "What can I do with my hair that will make it easy to care for by myself?" She responded slowly as she never gave me any credit in the hair department; in fact she always laughed at me when I did my own hair. It would usually turn out flat and she would say I looked like Doris Day from the 50's.

She finally suggested she'd cut it quite short and I could wear it straight; that would mean just washing and blow-drying it every morning. To my surprise I loved my new hairstyle and Dan and I eventually saved money by cutting each other's hair. He would go to the barber every few months and Doris would give me a good haircut whenever I got to Riverdale. But gradually all my frosting had grown out and I was dark and drab looking. While in Springfield, during my turning 40 crises, I had tried color shampoo but was never too pleased with it.

In Lake Zurich last summer I decided I would frost my hair myself. So with Vonnie's help we did it and it turned out well. I was a blonde again and it was more fun. I could cut and color my own hair and I didn't have to depend on a beauty shop. Of course it wasn't quite the same as when Doris did it but I was independent and saving money at the same time.

So I was thankful in Fort Wayne that I did have my hair short and it was easily taken care of, as my busy schedule began to take shape. I also continued to cut my own hair and I'm the barber for Dan and Mike too. I even cut Vonnie's hair right before school started and it looked cute, which is to say if you didn't look too closely and notice all the uneven ends.

But here I am on this dismal Monday morning needing a frosting and looking my age. It's noon now and I've walked Tuffy (very therapeutic for me along with my crocheting and knitting) and baked some cookies. Now

Erika is waiting for me to color with her. So, I know I'll survive and be happy again.

January 1, 1977

My goodness where did all my good intentions about writing in my journal every other week go? Here it is the first day of the new year and while in my heart I've made a few New-Year resolutions I'll make no promise to myself how often I'll jot down anything in my journal. My big excuse for waiting almost two months to write is that I've been busy but really I haven't been in the mood either.

November proved to be cold and snowy. Dan and the kids received their first report cards. Mike could have done better in a few subjects but Dan and Vonnie both had A averages.

We went to Highland, Indiana (Dan's brother's house) over Thanksgiving and stayed for four days. It was quite an ordeal as we took Tuffy and both kittens with us. I felt sorry for my sister-in-law Jan for putting up with us but she came through it all well. Tuffy of course slept with us and the cats had my nephew's playroom to themselves. All the kids slept on the floor in the front room.

Dan preached at his home congregation in Whiting that morning. It was the first time he had preached there. I could see how proud his parents were of him and there were many tear filled eyes after the service as Rev. Bradac introduced him to the congregation. "Here's a boy who was confirmed and baptized here in this church. Because of ill health, he gave up schooling for the ministry years ago but now is completing it." Rev. Bradac, the retired pastor in Whiting, is 87 years old and officiated at the marriage of Dan's parents 52 years before. We had Thanksgiving turkey dinner at Dan's sister's house (Amy).

The Friday after Thanksgiving we went to our old neighborhood (Riverdale) and visited with the Foyuts. Then on Saturday we drove to Lake Zurich. We had a fast visit with Pastor and Ruth Krueger, also with church friends the Hadlers and Harnacks. We even went back to "our farm" and after visiting with the people living in "our house" we went into the barn to see all "our cats." It made me sad to see them living out there and not on the back porch where we had fixed beds for them. Dan didn't even recognize our baby Whitey as she was so big and I am not sure the cats knew who we were. I almost wished we hadn't gone back; it would probably have been better to remember them the way it used to be.

On Sunday we attended St. Paul Lutheran Church in Dolton (our home church) and found it so good to see a lot of our old friends. We were surprised and thrilled to see in the church bulletin that they were going to have a food shower for us.

The few weeks between Thanksgiving and Christmas went by rapidly. I was just getting used to my working schedule again when it was time for another break. Two weeks this time. I had spent the interval in a hectic manner, working, shopping and going to the laundromat.

All the homes I cleaned were decorated so beautifully and as I worked I'd daydream about the next Christmas when we'd have our own home and be settled like most people.

We had put up our small artificial tree the week after Thanksgiving and it looked pretty good although each year it had less lights on it. All the decorations made the living room crowded and the tree was a glowing temptation to our kittens as, to our dismay, they attacked (even climbed) the tree early every morning while we were asleep. We practically had to redecorate every morning. When my parents came the situation changed but that's for later.

Our house was home though and we loved it all dressed up with Christmas Cards received, the tree, and our snow village scene on top of the hutch. The girls and I spent several hours baking favorite Christmas cookies too, which really put us in a holiday mood.

I sent my Christmas cards out early so our friends would know where we were this year. One girlfriend (we had grown up together) wrote she was anxious for us to settle down too as she had one full page in her address book just devoted to the Dan Kacers. We received so many greetings from friends and sometimes gifts of money. We heard from friends in Minnesota and in Lake Zurich besides all our regular Christmas correspondents. And of course our home church was more than generous as the different organizations sent us gifts in addition to the food shower. We also got an appreciated gift from our adopted church in Delavan, Illinois. Yes, the Lord was certainly taking care of us through His people. As an average family we bickered and disagreed with each other but we all loved each other too and knew how fortunate we were.

Gram and gramp Lindstrom arrived here a week before Christmas, stopping in Dolton first and bringing with them all our goodies from the food shower. There was enough to start a small grocery store, coffee, flour, sugar, canned goods, cake mixes, etc. We were set until our next move except for bread, milk and such. Also, we bought a quarter of a side of beef right after Thanksgiving so we wouldn't have to worry about meat for a while either.

"I have a nice roast which I'll take out of the freezer when Carol (my sister) and Harry come," I told my mom after we all kissed and became oriented to each other again. "Carol has her own meat and I don't like roast so I'll buy a ham," my mother replied in a typical motherly fashion. Even though I was 41, I was the daughter and my parents would continue to treat me as their youngest girl (the baby). But I get along with my mom in the kitchen as I just talk right back to her and remind her how motherly she is being. We all loved having my parents with us again, especially Erika, as she'd run to get a deck of cards the minute my mother walked in the door. They were always playing some kind of game.

My mom and dad had arrived on Friday, December 19th. The following Monday my sister and her husband along with their youngest daughter Amy came for a two-day visit. We had ham and all the trimmings after which we opened our gifts from each other that first night. Then Carol and Harry retired to a nearby Holiday Inn. They wanted to be alone. Amy slept with the girls.

The next morning, Tuesday, Erika and I went with the Elliott's to visit my cousin Deanna and her family in Bowling Green, Ohio, which was about 90 miles away. Mom and Dad had already been there just recently, the kids were still in school and Dan had studying to do but the rest of us went for the day. We had a great time visiting and eating. On the way home I wondered how I'd ever work again; this lady of leisure stuff was easy to take.

Carol, Harry and Amy left on Wednesday morning. We spent the next few days doing last minute shopping, baking and cleaning. I knew I was eating and drinking too much during this time but I vowed to start my diet again soon – sound familiar?

Gram and Gramp had Mike's room. He slept on the couch the 10 days they were with us. But Christmas Eve, I guess he felt Santa wouldn't come (at age 14?) if he were sleeping right next to the tree so that night he slept on the girls' bedroom floor.

My parents were very upset because the cats were ruining our furniture and were sleeping with the girls. It didn't help to argue that I had grown up always having several cats and a dog as pets. We kept the cats in the basement, years ago. They never received rabies or distemper shots as Fatty and Skinny did and the dog always slept with either my sister or me.

Also, gram took a magazine and hit the cats with it every time they went near the tree. Fatty was so frightened of my mom she rarely came into the parlor the 10 days they were there. She'd just hear gram's voice and down the hall she'd fly.

Gramp was up early every morning. He discovered, one early dawn, that we had "roaches" in the kitchen. I was devastated, as I had always associated these with dirty old houses. Now I prided myself with keeping the house clean (this was my profession for the year). The house was new but nevertheless we had them. Most of them were very small but we pulled the refrigerator and stove out from the wall and sprayed. As I write this, we haven't seen any for several days.

About the same time this was happening Dan took the cats to the vet for their second distemper and rabies shots. When he came home he stated, "The kittens have fleas" which wasn't surprising. He proceeded to put flea powder on Tuffy and our feline friends. We all began to itch between the roaches and fleas. My dad remarked to Dan, "You probably have fleas in your beard too." Dan had started a beard and mustache right after Thanksgiving but promised to shave it off before graduation. He was having his last fling and said the more remarks we made about it the longer he'd keep it.

We had a quiet Christmas with my parents right in Fort Wayne. On Christmas Eve our neighbors, Jerry and Barb and the landlord, Bill and his wife Betty had come over for eggnog and goodies. We all had gone to the 7pm children's service and Dan went again to the midnight service with Bill and Betty. Christmas morning the kids let us sleep until 8am. As usual Santa was too good to them and we were all in good spirits. We even had bought gramp something he needed for a change – a tape holder for his van.

The weatherman (Earl Finkel) had promised snow for Christmas but the sun was shining when we woke up and it continued to shine all day. But I guess the Christmas snow was just late, as we got up Sunday morning to a few inches on the ground with it still coming down.

Right after the first church service at Suburban Bethlehem we took off (slowly because of the weather) for Uncle Mike's house in Highland. My mom and dad stayed behind to animal sit which made our trip so much more enjoyable. Sunday night we had another Christmas with gram and gramp Kacer, Uncle K. O., Aunt Amy, brother Mike and his family. Dan's sister Anne even stopped in for a short while with her friend John and announced they were getting married. She had been divorced for several years and had four grown sons.

Monday brought us together again with our good friends and ex-neighbors, the Foyuts and Bochmanns. We were delighted a few weeks earlier to hear that Mariann Bochmann, Erika's godmother, was engaged. So it was good to see her and Rich and congratulate them in person.

We arrived home Tuesday afternoon through more snow and my parents left on Wednesday. They planned to go to my sister's house for New Year's and leave there a few days later for their home in Florida. Then they wouldn't be back until it is time for our next move.

Our "call service" we have heard will be April 27th or the 28th so we were anxious for the New Year to come. Dan preached at Suburban Bethlehem at the 7pm service on New Year's Eve. We then welcomed 1977 in with popcorn, pizza and pop.

On New Year's Day our friend and Dan's classmate Greg Fiechtner. came over for dinner. Greg had been the vicar in Barrington last year; a town right next to Lake Zurich.

When we woke up yesterday, because of the cold weather, there was no water as the lines were frozen. Dan made several trips with Bill, back and forth from his house, carrying water to us in 5-gallon containers. Do you realize how much water it takes to wash an average sink of dishes or flush a toilet just once? You don't until you have no water. Greg even brought us water from the dorm and we managed to survive the day as we had the day before. But it took me two hours to do the dinner dishes.

And now at bedtime I realize that tomorrow is the last day of vacation. On Monday everyone goes back to school but in a way I think they'll be glad. Mike stated he's bored and will be happy to get back and I know Dan wants to get started on our last lap until finishing time

.

January 2, 1977
Just a few lines today to say we have water again and what a treat. It came on after church. Dan and I both shouted to each other from opposite parts of the house that we heard it running and left the faucets dripping. We are to continue to let them drip this way in this very cold weather.

We took the tree down two days ago because the cats had it almost torn apart. Today we put everything else away. The house looks so bare after Christmas; the front room so forlorn, the hutch so vacant after the village was removed.

I took the Christmas tablecloth off the kitchen table and put the brown, yellow and white plastic one back on. It reminded me of Riverdale because that's where we were living when we bought it. Riverdale is where we lived for almost 10 years – before Springfield for 10 months followed by 2 months in Richmond, Minnesota, then a year in Wauconda, Illinois and now Fort Wayne, Indiana. Where next? I'm growing impatient.

January 28, 1977
I took Tuffy out for a walk and found it impossible to be out for more than 30-40 seconds at a time. The reason – it is 11 below 0 and the wind is blowing at 39 miles per hour making it a wind chill of 70 below 0. This hasn't been the first of bad storms that have hit Fort Wayne and surrounding areas this winter. It all began three weeks ago when on a Sunday night we

received 5" of snow. The kids were out of school for the first three days of the week and needless to say we all went house crazy. The following week (of January 16) they were both off on Monday and Vonnie was off again on Tuesday due to the extremely cold temperatures. For several days it had been below 0 and it had even dipped down to 25 below one night.

I had teased the kids on Monday as they had finally gone back to school, "This is the first Monday in three weeks I'll have a restful day off to myself!" Of course, I had Erika home but that was normal. Little did I know what the end of the week would bring?

On Wednesday at 3 o'clock when I went to pick Vonnie up from school the blowing snow was so bad I couldn't see right in front of me. I felt like I was suddenly riding in the clouds and when I saw the lights of an oncoming car I could only move over slightly. But it was just enough to get stuck in a snow bank. Luckily it was another sem student in the other car and he was kind enough to get me out of the snow bank. So of course the kids were off school yesterday (Vonnie's 12th birthday) and again today. Yesterday was cold but sunny so I did go to work. Then last night we all went out for pizza to celebrate birthdays – Vonnie's on the 27th and mine on the 22nd. The temperature was a warm 12 above 0. I made it a practice to faithfully listen to Earl Finkel; WOWO's weatherman (also WIND's in Chicago) so I knew it was to get much colder.

As I woke up this morning I could hear the wind howling around the house and the radio announced we had 4" of new snow during the night. Allen County was calling for a snow emergency and telling anyone who didn't have to go out to stay home. So, to my disappointment I couldn't go to work and it's my big day for doing two houses. Dan did venture to the sem and Mike went with him to play basketball at the gym. I just called there and all classes have been cancelled so they should be coming home soon.

I probably won't be able to work tomorrow either and just when I'm anxious to save money. I decided a few weeks ago that we all need a vacation and Easter in about 10 weeks would be a good time to go away. Now that Christmas is over I feel I can save part (a small part) of my earnings each week. I've even put my birthday money away; I need a trip more than anything. I have been trying to limit my trips to the grocery store and also have been going to the laundromat just once a week and washing some clothes out by hand in between time. I also buy oleo instead of butter and use only two scoops of coffee per day, avoid buying furniture polish, bleach, etc. – things I can get along without. My furniture may be spotted and our whites may be drab but I'm saving.

And now when I was doing so well I'm missing so many days of work. What's this to mean? Should I give up my struggle to save for a vacation for my family?

They just announced that all highways are closed in Fort Wayne and to please stay home. Why doesn't Dan call or come home? When I called there I didn't talk to him but to a classmate. Dan promised to call when he arrived (which he didn't) and again when he left for home.

Vonnie is getting anxious for him to call too as he's to pick up one of her girlfriends on his way home. She's supposed to have a party with four of her friends coming for an overnight. Originally they were to come home with her from school but it doesn't look like the party will come off at all the way things stand now. So, we'll have plenty of sloppy joes, fries, Jell-O and cake and ice cream over the weekend.

It looks like there's no improvement in sight in the weather department as we'll have sub-zero temperatures, winds and snow showers for the next three days. I like snow but enough of this cold weather. WOWO just called their sister station WIND in Chicago (my favorite) and things are the same there; I guess all of the mid-west is suffering. Even Florida wasn't left out in the crazy weather pattern as they received some snow too, last week. My mom called us (on my birthday) from Key Largo where they were visiting for a few days and said they had some snow in New Port Richey, where they are renting. And now for some strange reason my thoughts are all on Spring.

February 5, 1977

It is Saturday night and I am anxious to go to church tomorrow morning as last week it was closed. Of course, Vonnie didn't have her party last Friday night (a week ago) and when we tried to go for eggs last Saturday (across from our church) we couldn't get closer than ½ mile. Huge snowdrifts covered the road from Route 33 all the way to the church. So we weren't surprised when it was announced on the radio that Suburban Bethlehem was closed. Many other churches were closed last Sunday too but not because you couldn't reach them but because of the energy crisis. Places of entertainment were encouraged to close over the weekend and grocery stores were asked to shorten their hours. Even the laundromat was closed all weekend.

It's a good thing I had made arrangements with Lorna Wentzel to have my clothes washed at her house. Twice a week on my way to work I'd take her our wash and pick it up on my way home or the next day. I'm paying a small amount each load and will take her eggs each week too. Dear Lorna who insisted she would do the clothes, just as a favor, how I wish I could pay her what it's worth for me not to have to run to the laundromat.

Vonnie didn't have school again all week. Because of the energy crisis, all schools were closed Monday through Wednesday this week so Mike went back on Thursday to a school with the thermostat set down to 60.

I didn't work Tuesday or Wednesday (because all the kids were home in the houses I would have cleaned) so I've been quite idle and depressed. Then it snowed another 2" on Wednesday night so Suburban Bethlehem was closed again on Thursday and Friday. But I was determined to work on both these days even though it was beginning to snow as I drove to work. And it continued to snow all morning.

It's good I had left the girls home because when I came out from my Friday house I was completely stuck in a snowdrift in the drive. Dan was thrilled when I called him at the seminary cafeteria to give him the news. We eventually got unstuck but it took half an hour and a good Samaritan's help with a load of sand.

Yesterday's snowfall added four inches to what was already on the ground but what beautiful big drifts we have all around the house. Today we got through to buy eggs so I think we can get to church tomorrow. Also the weatherman is predicting temperatures in the 40's on Tuesday. What a mess we'll have!

Oh and I can't forget to add I'm still trying to build up our Florida fund. And all the more now since I heard from my mom today; it seems they have purchased a house down there with three bedrooms, a parlor, family room, kitchen and a large screened-in porch. They may be in by March 1st so we'll just have to visit and see their new home.

Saturday February 26, 1977

Now it is just a waiting game; waiting for five weeks until Easter vacation when we'll hopefully go to Florida and then waiting for April 29th, the date of our call service. After that we'll be waiting for graduation at the end of May.

In June we'll be leaving here for places unknown. I guess then we'll want time to stand still or creep by slowly as we move into our new house and get settled in our own congregation. But now the children and I are very conscious of time. Sometimes we comment to each other that the time has gone so fast this past six months in Fort Wayne that it's scary. Yet it seems to me that Florida is still so far off – five weeks from today.

I'll admit I've been obsessed with saving money for this trip. I'm really tight when I go to the store and try to buy just the necessities. I seem to bake every day though as the kids always want a treat, peach crisp, apple pie or a cake. I feel it's economical to keep flour, sugar, yeast, etc., in the house to bake rather than buying a lot of expensive goodies at the grocery store. While speaking of extras Dan and Mike got desperate for goodies last night and went to the store with their own money. They came home with a gallon of vanilla ice cream. Oh, and a 6-pack of root beer. Wow, but did it ever taste good!

Our big siege of cold is over. In fact, all of February has been warm with a few days even up to 60. So the outside is ugly, dirty and messy. Most of the snow is gone (that is until today) and there are pools of water all over. What an ordeal each time we go in and out with boots, rags to wipe Tuffy's feet and newspapers spread at the door. And I'm still mopping the floor several times a day.

Then this afternoon with just a few patches of snow here and there it began to snow again. The girls and I went to the library and the snow began to get heavy. After going to the grocery store we started out for home. It was a slow ride back as the roads were getting slick and the visibility was poor. Two hours later and it's still snowing. They're predicting 4" as winter isn't over yet.

As I grow older and Dan gets closer to this goal I realize how much I have in this life. I'm reading a book right now (one of Dan's) called *Free Fall.* It's about a Christian woman dying of cancer. She states in one part how when you're aware of your impending death in just so many months or a year, each day becomes so precious. As hard as it is I try, most of the time, to feel now, without knowing when I'll die, that each day is precious. I look at my family and thank God every single day for keeping us healthy.

We need our health and strength for the busy days ahead. Our ultimate goal (or should I say Dan's goal) is to serve the Lord and His people, because a minister is a servant of God.

We're human too as we anxiously await our vacation. Gram writes she has plenty of room for us but do we realize how far New Port Richey is from Fort Wayne?

March 9, 1977
My Aunt Louise died last Wednesday. When I received the news a flood of memories rushed across my mind. Now Louise wasn't actually my aunt but my mother's first cousin making her my second cousin. She was about three years older than my mom so naturally my sister and I always called her Aunt Louise and her husband Uncle George.

Louise and George had one child, a daughter Gail. She is just a little older than me so I spent a lot of time with her as we grew up. Gail and I went to the show quite often in those days (30 years ago) and we saw many horror movies. Then we'd come back to Gail's house and reenact the movie. Many times we'd use Aunt Louise's high back dining room chairs for part of our props, as those chairs looked just like the ones in which the heroine would sit while the villain hypnotized her. What imaginations we had!

Louise and George loved to entertain and had many friends, including my parents. Remember, this was pre-TV days so quite frequently several couples would get together for cards or for a party.

I know I loved sleeping at their house during the summer as Louise would let Gail and I sleep out on their screened-in porch at the back of the house. We never worried about someone peeking or breaking in on us and when you're young the floor doesn't seem hard. And I was thrilled when at the tender age of 8 Louise served me iced tea; I felt so grown up.

I remember my family vacationing with Louise, Gail, my mom's girlfriend Rena her daughter Elaine and my cousin Jean, for two weeks at Flint Lake near Valparaiso, Indiana when I was 10-years old. The dads all had to work all week and came on the weekends so our cottage was always busy and fun.

One weekend my mom's youngest sister Esther came with her little ones, Deanna Lee (4) and Jackie (3). Louise, loving children, played with and teased them and somehow acquired the name, "The Boss Lady." Then she in turn called them Daisy and Dopey Dilendot. I remember how Louise loved to shop. She'd go downtown (Chicago loop) on the bus and spend the day. It always amazed me that she spent several hours in just one store. Naturally, when we had a big snowstorm 10 years ago Louise and Gail were downtown doing their thing. John, Gail's husband, met them at the train station that night to walk them home through the huge drifts. The train that normally took one hour from the loop took several hours that night.

Louise loved to be hip and keep up with the times. She loved Mel Torme years ago when he was called, "The Velvet Fog" and she said she drooled when he sang. Then when the song **Cement Mixer Putty Putty** came out she kept getting mixed up and called it **Concrete Mixer Hubba Hubba.** She was talented too and made many gorgeous afghans and in later years some beautiful Christmas ornaments.

I can't forget she was brave too as I think about our chickens. During the second World War my dad raised chickens (right in the city) and one rainy day they forgot to come in out of the rain. We had planned a picnic that day but because of the downpour we all ended up at our house for an indoor picnic. The chickens lived in the garage but could also go outside through a hole and down a ramp in our back yard. It rained and it rained and they sat outside getting soaked. My mom was petrified of chickens and my dad was at work so I started to put a few of the chickens back into their shelter. Then Louise began to help and soon had put most of them back, although I think she was afraid too. And to this day I wonder why we bothered – it didn't hurt the chickens to get wet if they were too dumb to come in out of the rain.

Louise was short and a little overweight, but she always looked sharp. I thought she was sophisticated or maybe even a little dramatic. Dan put it another way – he said she was elegant.

So I was deeply saddened when she died at the age of 70 but the last three years of her life had been sad ones. She lost her husband, Uncle George, three years ago and she had never been quite the same after that. She made a small comeback at one time and went to California with my parents but then broke her hip a little over a year ago. She really never recovered from the broken hip and all its complications and died in a nursing home.

My cousin Gail said at the funeral she would be looking through her mom's things in a few weeks and was giving all the friends and family a keepsake of her mother's such as a cup or plate, etc. I'll be happy to get a keepsake but even without one I'll never forget my Aunt Louise.

March 22, 1977

We woke up this morning to 4" of snow on the ground and it was still snowing and blowing. I had gotten Mike out of bed already when I realized how nasty it was outside. So when we heard the school closings, including Concordia Lutheran High, Mike jumped back into bed. So, I have an unexpected day off work and the children are to be home all day to fight, eat and lay around. Vonnie just baked a cake and all three kids are fighting to see who gets to lick the bowl.

Dan is lucky as he made it to the sem although it took him at least a half hour to shovel, rock and slide his way out of our little Short Drive to the highway. I'm scheduled for a class tonight at the sem but don't know if they'll have it or not. I'll have to use Dan's car if I go as mine (my mom's) has the snow tires off already.

This week starts banquets for the graduates and their wives. This Thursday there's one just for the wives at a church in New Haven given by the LWML (Lutheran Women's Missionary League). Also next Sunday there's one at the Imperial House and on April 17th another one at the Marriott.

And, we'll be leaving for Florida in just a little over a week. We're all ready!

April 13, 1977
Jesus Christ is ris'n today Alleluia
Our triumphant holy day Alleluia
Who did once upon the cross Alleluia
Suffer to redeem our loss Alleluia
We sang loudly and happily, as it was Easter morning April 10, 1977.

Yes, we were celebrating the raising of our Lord from the grave after many long weeks of Lent and we were thankful. But we were over 1,000 miles from where we had spent it last year. Easter 1976 found us on our Wauconda farm on vicarage with Dan preaching at the sunrise service and here we were this year in New Port Richey, Florida, at the 8am service with my parents. We were to pack up and leave, right after church, for home. We were even anxious to get back (although we did have a wonderful week) so Dan could finish his last five weeks of school. The call service was only 2-1/2 weeks away.

We left our Fort Wayne home with the destination of Florida on Friday, April 1st at about 11:30 am. Dan drove the first 10 hours. To save time, I packed a lunch and we ate as we traveled.

We hit Louisville, Kentucky, right at the rush hour and saw Nashville, Tennessee, all lit up at night. We spotted the Grand Olde Opry by all the spotlights streaming from it.

We had Kentucky Fried Chicken for supper in a small town called Cave City, appropriately located in the Commonwealth of Kentucky. We had to ride around a while before we found the Colonel's; in fact Dan had to ask a policeman for directions. With a little bit of an accent the policeman said, "Straight ahead after a few miles you'll come to a red light, take a right and within a few blocks you'll be there." When we reached the light and came to a stop, Vonnie asked, "Is this a regular light?" Getting a positive reply she went on in a puzzled tone, "But how did he (the policeman) know the light would be red?" We all laughed and laughed, as she had only heard it called a stoplight, or traffic light; never a red light.

We could have made it to my parent's home on Saturday afternoon but after driving all night (I drove from 10pm until 10am) we were all tired, crabby and dirty. So we decided to stay overnight in Tallahassee to rest up and see some of the capital city of Florida.

Some sort of celebration was going on because as we tried to reach our motel we were blocked for a while by a parade. Later in the afternoon as we rode around, the traffic was congested and crowds were milling around all sorts of exhibits; stands selling wares and entertainment groups – all in the downtown area. So we visited an exciting, happy Tallahassee and found all of it quite beautiful with its gorgeous flowers and thick foliage. I felt like I was in Hawaii, although I've never been there.

The hills in the city reminded me of San Francisco (I've been there). We rode up and down the hills that night going to Barnaby's for supper and to Howard Johnson's for dessert. I had said I would treat for dessert thinking everyone would get an ice cream cone after a big meal. But no, nothing less than an ice cream sundae would do so dessert ended up costing as much as supper. We would have to be careful so we would have money left for the rest of our vacation.

We arrived at my parent's house about 5pm (after being lost because Dan hadn't taken directions down correctly). We attended Palm Sunday services before we left the capital city, in a beautiful Lutheran church. The church was set back off the road and was shaded with a variety of large shimmering trees.

Our six days spent in Florida consisted of eating too much, visiting and going to Disney World, Busch Gardens and Tarpon Springs. We also managed to have some time on the beach.

The weather was gorgeous on Monday but on Tuesday when we ventured to Disney World it was cold. But that didn't put a damper on our fun nor did the fact that the park was packed – we expected that. It wasn't unusual to stand in line for a ride or exhibit for 30-40 minutes but the crowds were controlled and everyone was polite so you didn't mind waiting.

On Thursday when we went to Busch Gardens the lines weren't quite so long and the weather was warmer. It was fun walking through the beautiful gardens, seeing all the wild animals from the sky ride or monorail and refreshing to get a free glass of beer at the Anheiser-Busch building.

The two older children (Mike and Vonnie) enjoyed the roller coaster (it has a fancy name) more than anything. We sat and watched them whirl down the track and stand on their heads twice. Vonnie then had the nerve to say, right after the ride, that it hadn't been too bad – at which Mike asked her, "Then why were you screaming?"

On Friday we went to Tarpon Springs where they dive for sponges and played the tourists as we oohed over all the lovely shell necklaces. Then we were on to Howard Beach just a few miles further on the Gulf where we had been on Monday. I spent most of the time there picking shells up off the sand. Most of them were small but we would still make something out of them. Then Dan and I walked around the entire beach at the shoreline with the water lapping at our feet. We all were getting red if nothing else and we were relaxed and happy even though our money was just about gone. Of course, gram and gramp wouldn't let us spend much while we were there. "You'll need it to get home," my mom kept insisting.

The children colored eggs Saturday afternoon and we had a cookout with friends at suppertime. Toward dusk we enjoyed lounging and visiting with each other out on my parent's screened-in porch. Many of the houses in Florida have these screened-in areas and because of the climate are more like another room than a porch.

But all too soon it was all over. We went to church Easter morning and then went back to the house and loaded the car for home.

We drove all day Sunday and Monday to get home about 8:30 Monday night. We loved the mountains and foothills in Georgia, Tennessee and Kentucky, and we even drove up to *Look-Out Mountain* in Chattanooga and marveled at the view.

So, we have been home for two days now but I don't go back to my house cleaning jobs until Friday. So I have a few more days to relax, unwind and catch up on things.

The kids and Dan are back in school. I shopped for groceries yesterday, wrote letters and picked up around the house. We're all back to our normal routine, for the next two weeks anyway; then we'll be moving again to our new house.

Sunday April 24, 1977

I've been nervous and restless the past several days, pre-call and moving jitters I guess. I can't even sit still long enough to watch one of my half hour soap operas and for me that's unusual as I consider myself a soap opera addict. I think my love for them stems back to the days when I used to listen to them on the radio with my mother's mom – grandma Decker. She lived with us from the time I was 4 (when my grandpa died) until she died when I was 19. She was a rare wonderful person and I'm glad I picked up some habits from her.

One of these habits was my love for the soap operas and a passion for baking with yeast. But gram, without much of an education, maybe up until the 7th grade, was a whiz at spelling and arithmetic and could sing such beautiful harmony. I sadly regret I didn't inherit any of those traits.

I remember going to the corner store with my grandma. There were no supermarkets then and she'd have all the items purchased, added up in her head, before the clerk even began to add them up on paper. She could spell most anything; maybe the old spelling bees of years ago should be used more often today. Grandma washed clothes every Monday; it took her all day with a wringer machine and no dryer. Then all day Tuesday she'd iron and listen to "Our Gal Sunday," "Ma Perkins" and "Young Widower Brown" to mention just a few.

It seems my mom never got too interested in the shows as she was working out of the home quite a lot. In 1954, one of my favorite shows "The Guiding Light" was put on TV. What fun to see all the characters in person after just listening to them for years. But gram never really appreciated television and was always afraid to change the channels. I think she still preferred her shows on the radio up until the time of her death. Also, she loved Saturday night barn dances on the radio. Wouldn't she have been thrilled with *Hee Haw* on TV some 30 years later?

Every Saturday was chili and homemade bread day. Mom, home for a change, would make the chili while gram baked her delicious bread. Fond memories find my sister and me coming home from a Saturday afternoon football game to the aroma of homemade bread, which had been raised, on the old-fashioned type radiator. Until this day every time I bake bread or coffee cake I yearn for a radiator of yester year.

But enough of my rambling. Now that the call service is just five days off I feel a little more relaxed. Wally and Zelda are coming this Thursday night (for the service on Friday morning) and we are having some surprise company too.

John Riske (the Rev.) called us last Thursday night from his sister's home in New Orleans, Louisiana. He and Lois and the children will be passing through here just in time for the service on their way back to their congregation in Hale, Michigan. So, we have an exciting week coming up. I'll be working Monday through Thursday and with getting everything ready for company I won't have time to be restless. I feel like John and Lois were just graduating from the sem in Springfield and that was two years ago.

Dan said right after he entered the seminary, "I'm anxious to get these four years out of the way so I can go out and do the Lord's work." And here we are right at the door. There's one thing that never can disappoint you and that's the passing of time. As that old song goes, "Time Waits for No Man."

Another Blackie
Monday April 25, 1977
As we creep (now the time is going so slow) toward the day for which we've all been waiting, I thought I'd like to put down a few words about our new cat Blackie. This time Blackie is a male about the same size as our two females.

Blackie showed up one morning on our back porch, right after we came home from Florida. I told Dan since "Be Kind to Animal Week" was coming up in May I just had to feed him. And of course because it got cold at night, Yvonne and I made him a bed out of a cardboard box filled with an old sheet and bedspread.

Every morning when I get up (even before starting the coffee) I feed Skinny, Fatty and of course Blackie, who would be peeking in our kitchen glass sliding doors. Dan's just a little mad because we can't let our cats outside. They've been in heat more than not lately and Blackie is always around. Although at times we think he has another home because sometimes he's gone for several hours and isn't always very hungry. So, he had to come from somewhere. I told Dan "I don't think he's that interested in our females – he's more anxious for us to hold him and give him affection" – he reminds me of Morris back on our farm with all his affection. I told Bill (the landlord) when he rents this house again to tell the new people it comes with a black, male cat. Although Tuffy sleeps and eats with his cat sisters he won't tolerate Blackie. He continues to bark at him just as he did our cats in Wauconda.

Monday May 16, 1977

I've finally made myself sit down and write again. Here it is two weeks after call service and so much has happened. Why is it that things never turn out quite the way you imagine or want them to? I kept picturing our call to be to a small lovely town and we'd be bestowed with a large old parsonage in which to live (with a fireplace of course).

When our call did come I went into shock as it was to a large suburb south of Chicago, just 15 minutes from our old home. Now maybe I should have been thrilled to be going back home but I wasn't. It could never be the same. I had cut the cord (slowly and painfully) three years prior and I didn't want to return to this area. We had requested Northern Illinois, which we got, but I guess Dan and I were both thinking of north of Chicago.

This was just one of the many factors involved. There was no housing (just an allowance) and Dan was to be an assistant – which would be fine if he were a younger man or the assistant to a pastor close to retirement age. But this would be to assist someone the same age.

Without going into detail Dan and I were both depressed and devastated over this call. We talked about it and prayed many prayers before Dan came to his final decision. He would have to decline the call.

As I mentioned, we had a lot of company for the call service; Wally and Zelda who stayed all weekend and John and Lois Riske and children, who had to leave on Saturday right after breakfast. Yet, I'm afraid my reaction to our call wasn't too grateful, even though we had company. The old devil (which is always inside) really came to the surface. I went through all kinds of phases, which Dan (as a counselor?) diagnosed as a crisis. A disappointment can act on your nervous system just as a death or illness does – Dan enlightened me.

I was sad, and then depressed but by Sunday afternoon (after Wally and Zelda left) I had accepted the fact that this was our call. I felt a burden lifted off me and I suggested to Dan that we go for a ride. Our ride ended up at another sem couple's home. They were going to Florida and had requested Texas. We talked and shared views and I felt much better.

But, Monday morning found Dan down and out and I was mad all over again. Then the searching began. I felt even more miserable as most of our classmates were thrilled with their calls; and some of their parsonages were huge. Their congregations sent them pictures.

On Friday night (call service had been that morning) we had all gone to a potluck at the Yungman's house, leaving the kids at home. Everyone was comparing notes but Dan and I were silent. We realized this was a divine call and we respected it. Dan acknowledged it and his intention to decline was not an overnight decision. He felt he could serve the church better in another area and capacity and wanted to go somewhere we could stay for a while.

So, now it's Monday, two-weeks later and graduation is this Friday. Many of our classmates will be leaving in a week or two, but we'll probably be here for a spell, as we don't know what the future holds for us. Maybe we'll get another call next week or it might be months before we hear anything. It's a chance we had to take.

We had our last banquet last night and it was a sad occasion. Four years ago I rebelled against the seminary and now I realize I'll really miss it. I've made so many friends and a lot of them just in this last year. We are all united because our lives have been the same these past few years. We've all struggled for survival (literally) and I guess we've grown used to it. How strange it will be without our clothes and food bank, our Seminette's Tuesday night class and our close friendships. Our lifestyle is really due for a big change.

A group of us went out for a drink after the last banquet and we decided we'd all try to keep in touch through the years. We'll be scattered from North Dakota to Florida and all in-between. One of the wives decided to hug all the gentlemen as she said her goodbyes; I guess she realized our time together was growing short. Eventually we all were hugging each other and there may have been some tears in the group.

Friday June 3, 1977

I'm weary of waiting, wondering and worrying. We still haven't heard anything of a new call and it's quite depressing as many of our classmates already have or are now leaving town.

Greg F., or as the kids call him – Barrington Greg (the vicar in Barrington when we were in Lake Zurich) left almost two weeks ago for California. His congregation is just a few hours from his parent's home and as a bachelor he has a house with three bedrooms.

The Hallman's left today and the Thompson's are leaving Sunday. I'm happy for them but must admit to being a little jealous. I am just so glad the Wentzel's and Yungman's will be here until the end of the month; sure hope we know something by then. The Larson's will be leaving on the 15th and I want to call them to say goodbye. They are the ones going to Florida. And the Messmons, Joan and Warren, will be headed to Connersville, IN soon.8

On June 12th we'll go to Michigan for Wayne Wentzel's ordination. We're all looking forward to this but again I have mixed emotions. Will Dan be ordained on the 26th of this month as scheduled? He has to have a call first.

I have so many people to write to but I have nothing to tell them yet. One, of course, is Charlie Liedl, my friend of years ago when I worked on the Santa Fe Railroad as a Courier Nurse. Charlie worked in the bus depot (which was actually the train depot) and always found time to meet each nurse as she arrived in San Francisco. We'd come into the depot on the bus that picked us up from the train in Oakland to take us across the Bay Bridge.

Charlie, who was about my father's age, always would be there to take us out for coffee and would invite us to visit him at his home in nearby San Mateo. No matter how many nurses Charlie brought home for a meal his wife, Bea, never seemed to mind. Even after I quit the railroad, Charlie continued to keep in touch. We've corresponded over the past 17 years and he had visited us several times in Riverdale. So it was thrilling last week to have him and his wife Bea visit us in Fort Wayne. They came in their mini-motor home and had been traveling all over the countryside since Easter. Charlie retired just recently and they love to travel. They plan to get home by the 4th of July.

Now I'm just one of the many ex-courier nurses Charlie still befriends. Dan and I were amazed, several years ago, at his book of statistics on us gals. He has the following information on most of us in his little black book, name, address, starting date, leaving date with the Santa Fe, when married, how many children, etc. He called a few of the girls from our house and you can imagine how many more calls and visits he would make on the way home. We just had two days to catch up on each other's news and when they left us headed for Chicago, then Wisconsin. I know they were getting anxious to get home too as their son Johnny was holding the fort alone.

Charlie had surgery last August, a leg amputation, and while he was with us really did well on his new artificial leg. We even had him walking up and down hills as we visited the seminary campus. At the same time that he was in the hospital last year, Dan and I had attended a Courier Nurse Reunion at my girlfriend Arlene's house. It was fun to see so many familiar faces after 17 years and we all thought of Charlie with devotion when we heard of his surgery

Dan had looked around at all of us for a few minutes and then had declared, "Why, you're all Charlie's Angels."

Well, back to the present. I'm so tired of cleaning other people's houses. I'm longing to belong somewhere and have a place of my own. If I sound like I'm lamenting, I am, and will not write again until I have something concrete to say.

June 9, 1977

We've heard. Dr. Eggold's secretary called Dan this morning and we received another call. Now for one who wanted to travel and to just leave this area, I must admit I was disappointed at first, because we were called just 20 miles from here.

But within hours the Circuit Counselor took us out to the church and I knew I'd love it. The church, St. Paul, is located five miles outside New Haven, Indiana, and it's a small country church with a beautiful wooden altar and pulpit. And the pulpit is on a pedestal!

Typically, there's a cemetery on one side of the church while a large old parsonage graces the other side. But the parsonage is now used as the Sunday School and has been for the past several years. So, we have to begin to look for housing, something we are quite used to by now. So I'm frustrated all over again as I know we'll stay in this house in Fort Wayne for a while yet. You can't rent or buy a house and get into it overnight.

I don't dislike living in this house, we've been here for almost a year and I've grown to love it and the area. I'll miss Bill, Barb, Jerry, but this is our student house and I want to move close to our new church.

I'll try to be patient.

June 21, 1977

We've looked at several houses and they are all so expensive. We saw one last night, about a country mile away from the church, which would be ideal but must not get my hopes up. This house also is quite expensive and as the church (congregation) will be buying the house, it's really up to them.

The Larsons left a week ago and Wayne Wentzel was ordained in Michigan on June 12th. We were able to make it to the ordination but couldn't make it the following Sunday to Ron Yungman's, as it was Father's Day and Dan had a preaching assignment in Burr Oak, Michigan. Both the Yungmans and Wentels will be leaving next week so we'll be the only ones left from our class. While I feel melancholy at times I guess we're lucky to be able to choose where we'll live.

My mom and dad have been with us for several days now and this morning they left for Riverdale, taking Mike and Vonnie with them. The kids will stay with my girlfriend Doris so they can be with their friends, Bobby and Gail, until next Sunday when we go to Dolton (next to Riverdale) for Dan's ordination. So things are moving along and Dan will be installed at St. Paul, Gar Creek, on July 10th but he'll start working on the first of the month.

I feel so bored at times just sitting and watching TV (I'm down to two jobs now) when I should be packing and cleaning. But we must wait for a moving date and of course a place into which we will move. During the past few weeks I have knitted six toilet paper toppers and read seven books. And I keep thinking happiness is a clothesline full of blowing clothes in my own back yard.

On June 16th a few lines out of my little book "God's Minutes" seems to aim right at our situation and they helped to strengthen me. "Teach us to take our joys as they come, and to make friends with our trials; to know that life is good, whatever skies it may please Thee to bring over us." M. O. Evans PHD, DD Cincinnati, Ohio

July 11, 1977

Dan was installed as St. Paul's pastor yesterday. It was a beautiful service and I was happy that we both had our parents with us for the occasion. A delicious potluck was served after the service. Speeches were made, we were entertained with music and everyone had fun. I realized as I sat there and later as I met so many of the members of the congregation (I'll never remember all their names) that no matter where you go people are pretty much the same; friendly and ready to hold out a welcoming hand.

I had planned originally to end my journal dramatically at call service but as I mentioned things weren't too settled at that point. Then, two weeks ago when Dan was ordained in Dolton I felt that this was the climax. We were thrilled that so many of our friends came for the service. Friends came from Lake Zurich; I still miss my farm and neighbors. Dear friends from Riverdale came, loving relatives came and even three gentlemen, whom we would soon know, came from Gar Creek.

Pastor Marquardt conducted the ordination. Pastor Dishop was the liturgist and Pastor Krueger, Dan's Bishop from Lake Zurich, was the preacher. Yes, this could have been the end, this was what Dan had been working toward but still I'm rambling on just a little longer.

Now, I'll backtrack just a bit. On July 2nd the children and I had gone to Havana (my sister's) with my parents for a week. I felt I needed a vacation and would enjoy being with my sister and her family. Dan stayed at home with the animals and conducted his first funeral on July 6th, even before he was installed.

Also while we were gone the voter's assembly voted to buy the house I had mentioned previously, the one down the street from the church. So now I can elaborate more on the house and add I'm very happy and excited. It's on an acre of land, as are all the surrounding ones. We're out in the country and yet we have a neighborhood. There are about 15 houses on Berthaud Road, extending from busy Route 24 all the way to the church (at least a mile). The house is a white two-story with aluminum siding. There's a parlor, dining room, a kitchen with a dining area, family room with a fireplace (yes we got our fireplace) and a half bath downstairs. Sliding glass doors lead from the family room outside. The yard is huge and all fenced in. Can you imagine Tuffy's delight? Upstairs are four bedrooms and a full bath. There's no basement but we have a 2-car garage.

All our waiting has come to a fruitful end. The Lord doth provide!

Our friends Lorna and Wayne Wentzel left almost two weeks ago. They were one of the last sem families to leave. But our turn is coming.

Our house on Short Drive is cluttered and dirty yet this hot weather doesn't give me the incentive to do any big cleaning. I'll wait until we move. I did wash the parlor furniture with blue luster and Dan did the rug today, but there's so much more to do. I've packed a few things but really can't do too much until we get the word that everything is clear with the title, etc. Dan takes a box of books out to his study in the old parsonage every time he drives out there.

I have so many people to write, with whom to share our good news and as I look back I know if we had to do it over again, we'd do everything the same way.

TUESDAY, SEPTEMBER 13, 1977

Erika started kindergarten last week and to my surprise she really seems to enjoy it. We've been in our beautiful new house for seven weeks already and we're so settled, two weeks ago we had an open house for the congregation.

Our congregation and neighbors, some of them the same, have really made us feel welcome here. Since we're out in the country surrounded by farms, besides receiving cakes, cookies and pies some have been supplying us with fresh fruits and vegetables too.

Albert and Mary Schlegel, who live three houses down with their two children Julie and Paul, actually have adopted us into their family. Mary amazes me the way she cooks, bakes and even has a big quilt frame set up right in her home which isn't unusual in this area. Maybe I'll learn to quilt.

Albert helped us move from Short Drive to Berthaud Road with his big white van. The girls and I were shopping when he came to help Dan with some of the furniture. Later he helped us move Fatty with 6 kittens and a pregnant Skinny.

Out of desperation I had so many fresh garden vegetables, I had to can some for the first time in my life. Of course, I had to have help from Mary who is into all that kind of things as Albert has a huge garden.

A month ago my beloved Aunt May in California died so my parents made an unexpected trip out there. Aunt May, my dad's sister, was the type of aunt that everyone would want to have. She'd give you the clothes off her back and sleep on the floor so you could have a bed. She was like a second mother to me; my life certainly will be emptier without her.

Then a few days later the music world was shaken by the death of Elvis Presley. He apparently suffered a fatal heart attack and this hit close to home as he was just two weeks older than me.

As I write, Vonnie just got on the bus in front of the house. She goes to Central Lutheran School in New Haven and is becoming friends with Julie Schlegel. Erika attends the same school and is in the afternoon kindergarten so she is still asleep. This is a consolidated school (3 churches) so it's quite large but the girls seem to be adjusting.

Mike will catch his bus in a few minutes for Woodlan High, a school of about 500, which is 2-1/2 miles from here. He's already playing football and making new friends.

Dan is kept busy at St. Paul with its 450 baptized members. We are close enough to the church to walk yet not right on top of it.

Our cat population exploded seven weeks ago (the day we moved). Fatty had six kittens and Skinny followed three weeks later with six, one of which died. So, now we are trying to find homes for 11 kittens. Just what I need!

But we're finally settled, happy and putting our roots down I hope in Gar Creek, Indiana. This area, which has a New Haven mailing address, is actually five miles outside of that town. It is affectionately called Gar Creek as, at one time, it was on its way to becoming a town but never quite succeeded.

I love being surrounded by wide-open spaces and marvel each time I look out the bedroom window and see all the cornfields. Now I know things won't always be a bed of roses because in the church you can't please everyone all the time. So we'll have to acquire thick skin and I'll remind Dan of what Pastor B (my sister's pastor from Havana, Illinois) told his Bible class one morning.

He said, "I've got calluses where people don't even have places."

So with a few added places or calluses and a continuing faith in the Lord we can do it. We can serve the Lord with free and happy hearts and with gladness because of what Jesus did for us many years ago.

Our family stayed in Gar Creek while Dan served St. Paul for 6-1/2 years. In 1984 he accepted a call to St. Luke in Plainfield, Indiana. This was followed by 8 years of service at St. John in Aurora, Indiana staring in 1992.

E P I L O G U E

Gar Creek – Another Chapter is Closed
January 1984

Our first knowledge of Gar Creek came in June of 1978 when Dan received a call to St. Paul Lutheran Church in New Haven, Indiana. Now, after 6 ½ years Dan has taken another call and it's time to leave our church, home, friends, and a part of ourselves behind, yet again.

As I look back it's been a wonderful time of my life although I guess I didn't always feel that way. So, I'll reminisce and try to put down, in some order, the times that stand out in my mind.

> ➢ Asking, "Who's that little fat boy on our couch?" The couch sitting on our front sidewalk in Ft. Wayne waiting to be loaded onto a moving truck. The Gar Creek congregation moving us to our new home. Learning the boy in question was Paul Schlegel.
> ➢ Mary Schlegel and Sandy Ball standing on the church steps introducing themselves to me. A shy, 13-year old Julie Schlegel standing next to her mother listening politely as I told her about Yvonne who was at my sister's house in Havana, Illinois.
> ➢ Mike choosing to go to Woodlan High School instead of continuing at Concordia so he could stay in sports. Driving him to football practice at 7:00 a.m. every morning, except Sundays, that first August.

- Yvonne thinking Central Lutheran School was too big, but later loving it and forming some precious friendships.
- Erika starting kindergarten at Central and getting on the bus each morning with Vonnie; the cornfields in the background.
- Dan playing golf and being co instigator with Arnie Ball of the Annual Gar Creek Open. The informal Adult Bible Discussion Group being formed as an extension of The Open.
- Mom going to Sunday School with the kids and teaching Nursery and Kindergarten classes for 6 ½ years. Singing in the choir for two years even though she had no voice.
- Walking a mile every morning with Mary Schlegel and Mary Werling, or riding bikes with Mary, Julie, Vonnie, and Erika and falling in the ditch.
- Getting snowed in for three days and Dan walking to the Hockemeyer farm for milk that would otherwise have been thrown away. . . Mary, Alf, Julie, and Paul digging their way through the snow to our house for Vonnie's 13th birthday.
- Tuffy walking over snow drifts that extended right over the fence and out of the yard. Being gone for a few hours but always finding his way back.
- Watching Mike play football, Von volleyball and basketball and both kids running track.
- Erika being thrilled with living in a neighborhood where she had other kids her age to play with, especially Sara Werling and Jill Hoeppner. Erika breaking her arm at the beginning of one summer.
- Enjoying a week each summer at Lake James – going out to eat, golfing, and then on the weekend going to the small theater in Angola with Mary and Alf. On Sunday having a beautiful service in the chapel followed by a famous Gar Creek pot-luck in the pavilion.
- Having mom and dad visit us from Florida and taking us to Washington D.C. one summer, and more recently to California.
- Planting and caring for a huge garden, learning to can vegetables to fill our pantry, and stripping and refinishing furniture in the Schlegel's garage.
- Teaching Bible School a week during the summer. Fun and games at the Youth Group Annual Ice Cream Social.
- Mike working at the Gar Creek Nursery each summer, for Fritz Meyer, with Conn Hermann and Brent (Dirv) Werling. Von hoeing in the hot sun with Lisa Hoeppner at The Beverly Nursery.

- Mike and Dirv doing exercises on the front lawn and then running for several miles.
- Von and Erika playing softball in Woodburn during the summertime.
- Our growing friendships with Pastor Ralph Wetzel and Sue, Mary and Albert Schlegel, Mary and Vern Werling, Sandy and Arnie Ball and Linda and Fritz Meyer, the Hockenmeyer families, and so many more.
- Mike graduating from high school and enrolling at IU/Bloomington. A feeling of emptiness when he left home for the first time.
- Taking weekend trips to Michigan, Chicago, and Pokagon State Park with Sue and Ralph.
- Mourning over the deaths of gramp and gram Kacer within 2 ½ weeks of each other.
- Getting a job at Ft. Wayne State Hospital and Training Center, at Carroll Hall, with Sue. Loving the kids (residents) but feeling too much pressure. Leaving after 13 months.
- Continuing to teach the little ones with Wendy, Julie, Rod, Vonnie, and Lisa. Missing Sunday School this past year because of the building program.
- Enjoying the annual Card Party, Ladies Aid Christmas Parties and all the other special occasions when we'd get together for fellowship and food!
- Mike coming home from school and greeting Dirv either over the phone or at the front door with an emphatic, "Dirve!", or making him laugh by yelling, "Hey Barbs, how about some lunch?"
- Erika going on a 7 mile hike with her Sunday School class as a marathon, originated by her teacher Carmen Zink. The money collected going to Missions.
- Mike writing home and telling us about Amy for the very first time.
- Vonnie going out with Randy, Mark, Barry, and then Curt but always enjoying her girlfriends too.
- 1980 – Celebrating St. Paul's 100th Anniversary, besides all the festivities, a building committee being formed.
- Vonnie placing 1st in many cross county races and track meets.
- Attending most of the funerals and weddings Dan performed at Gar Creek. Crying at the wedding of Elmer and Velma Werling the day after Thanksgiving. 1978. They were both in their late 60's at the time.

- Crying with Carol and the girls when my brother-in-law Harry died, after a brief illness, at the age of 50.
- Flying to Florida, alone for the first time, to be with mom while dad had plastic surgery on his buttocks due to a decubitus; one of the many complications he suffered after double hip surgery.
- The sadness and loneliness, at the end of the summer 1981, after having 14-year old Tuffy put to sleep due to heart failure.
- Vonnie being crowned queen and Dirv king of their junior prom. The proud parents of both taking pictures of the royal couple on the front lawn the next morning after church.
- Dan continuing to carry the load of teaching confirmation, preaching the word, and reaching out to the sick and shut-ins, besides being responsible for two field workers (seminarians) each year.
- Church being cancelled three weeks in a row one January due to snow and cold.
- Mike taking a job selling books during the summer of '82. After five weeks of knocking on doors in Escondido, CA, Mike quitting his job and going to Lynwood, CA to stay with Uncle Hermie.
- Mom and dad taking us to California in their van to pick-up Mike and having a little vacation at the same time.
- Dad encouraging me to go back to work, at State School, to help Mike out when a job became available at Carroll Hall, and his helping me buy a car in Havana.
- Working with the kids again at Carroll Hall but this time all alone, no Sue. Being scared many times at the responsibility of my job, but knowing the Lord was always with me.
- Erika playing basketball and volleyball and running track in the 5th grade. Making the softball All Star Team two years in a row.
- The shock and unreality of the shooting death of 19-year old Carmen Zink as she walked from her car to a local restaurant for a Christmas party.
- Continuing to get up each a.m. in the dark to go to work. Finally getting another nurse to work with me at Carroll Hall due to the Pal Program.
- Getting together, going out to eat with the parents of Lisa, Vicki, Gary, Mitch, Dirv, and Kelley to plan a "together" Graduation Party at Meyer's Barn.
- In April 1983, St. Paul finally deciding to build a much needed addition to the church (parish hall and narthex).

- Flying to Florida when dad was hospitalized and had to have dialysis. Dad suffering a stroke just a day after my arrival. Mom, Carol and I returning north in the van a week later, on the day of dad's death – May 18th.
- The moving of the old parsonage that stood next to the church, to a new location just ½ a mile away (while I was in Fl).
- Ground breaking for the church addition taking place on Sunday, May 23rd, just a day after Dan's birthday and my dad's burial.
- Vonnie and friends graduating in May from Woodlan High School. Vonnie being crowned Homecoming Queen in her senior year and looking forward to college at Ball State.
- Mike working for Nabisco with Conn during the summer of '83. Wearing dress clothes and driving me to work each morning so he could use the car.
- Vonnie babysitting for Markers again; saving as much as she is able.
- Our adopted cat Lou Lou (the Bum) finding his way home after being lost in Woodburn 7 weeks earlier.
- The shock, grief, and then unbelief of Dirv's death in a boating accident in Michigan. Most of us hearing the news on T.V. Mike running a mile home from a friend's house, in the dark, crying.
- The compassion and closeness of many of Dirv's friends as they gathered at our house. Bringing love and comfort, as best as we could, to Mary, Vern, Sara, Bruce and Matt that same night.
- The sixteen young pallbearers walking down the aisle; Dan giving us comfort in the words, "Brent has won the crown of victory."
- The line of cars in the procession extending all the way from New Haven to Webster Road off of Highway 14 (4 miles), giving us a feeling of humility. Our tears being dried for a short while as we realized what a task was for those still in the flesh.
- Walking to the church each evening with Mary Schlegel and checking on the progress of the Parish Hall. Pausing to say a little prayer at Dirv's grave.
- Dedicating our new addition on December 11th. Velma being able to be there, even though she's bedridden and being fed by a tube.
- Mom arriving from California via Amtrak just in time for Christmas, and freezing.
- -16 degrees weather on Christmas Eve forcing churches to cancel services, including ours. Going to Christmas morning services with a small attendance.

- Dan receiving and accepting a call to Plainfield, IN – a small town near Indianapolis.
- Visiting Plainfield, a second time, to check out the parsonage and then realizing we had too much furniture.
- Receiving expressions of love and friendship from our many friends as we prepared to move. A party at work for me; a pastor and wives get together at Hall's Guest House for Dan; meals at parishioner's homes and restaurants; a gorgeous quilt from a dear family; Walt Werling Sr. and children, an evening at the Vondran's turning into a surprise gathering of 10 couples and all this topped off by a huge potluck farewell in our new Parish Hall on Dan's last Sunday – January 29th.
- Thinking amidst tears, speeches, and songs sung by the choir, and parting embraces by many, how fortunate we had been in knowing such wonderful people.
- Our trip to Florida beginning with a slow start as Ft. Wayne was receiving 6" of snow. The weather being cool in New Port Richey, but relatively warmer than at home. Eating and drinking maybe a little too much; enjoying Sue and Ralph's company and bringing mom home with us.
- Sorting, cleaning, packing, and some crying as we emptied our home in Gar Creek after 6 ½ years.
- Mary and Albert venturing to Plainfield with us taking mom, Erika, and plants in their car. Our car loaded with more plants, misc. things, and Skinny in a cage.
- Settling into our new home, not really having time to miss friends in Gar Creek but feeling a void.
- Registering Erika in her new school (Van Buren) just down the hill. Finding the Post Office, Library, and a bank.
- Dan being installed with all of his family, and mom, here for the service and a luncheon following in the church basement.
- A snowfall in Plainfield bringing 9" to the area and closing the schools for 3 ½ days. Erika's sadness!
- Yvonne being here for Spring Break during another storm. Mike visiting more often. Gram staying with us several weeks after helping us move.
- Mom (gram) leaving for Florida with cousin Charlotte, Erika going to school, and Dan to the office. My being alone, depressed and in shock. Taking a shower, washing my hair, walking a mile, shopping with a new friend.
- I'm still coping.

January 2007

Dan retired in the summer of 2000 at the age of 65 and we moved back to Plainfield (Indianapolis area). At this time, Dan went on to serve 3 congregations as Interim Pastor.

He now continues to serve in the Intentional Interim Ministry.

Our children are married and we have 4 grandchildren, all in the Indianapolis area. Our lives are full and busy and we are thankful each morning for all the Lord's blessings.

www.ingramcontent.com/pod-product-compliance
Lightning Source LLC
Chambersburg PA
CBHW061310280526
45784CB00002B/950